All the Gentlemen Callers

Letters Found in a 1920's Steamer Trunk

Found and presented by
Judith Thompson Witmer

Also by Judith T. Witmer

Growing Up Silent in the 1950s,
Not All Tailfins and Rock 'n' Roll (2012)

Loyal Hearts Proclaim: A Historical Compendium
of Lower Dauphin High School, 1960–2010 (2012)

Hummelstown Celebrates 250 Years (Editor) (2012)

Jebbie: Vamp to Victim, The Truth about Miss Pifer

I am From Haiti: The Story of Rodrigue Mortel, MD

Je Suis D'Haiti: Par Rodrigue Mortel, MD

Moving Up! A Guide for Women in Educational Administration

Team-Based Professional Development
A Process for School Reform

The Keystone Integrated Framework: A Compendium

A Style Manual for Publications

How to Establish a Service-Learning Program

About the Author

Judith Thompson Witmer is a graduate of Curwensville High School and holds a B.A. in English Literature from Penn State, an M.S. in Humanities, a Doctorate in Educational Administration from Temple, and both graduate and post-doctoral credits from Harvard University.

A former high school English teacher, principal, central office administrator at Lower Dauphin School District, adjunct professor for Temple University's Graduate School, and currently Director of the Capital Area Institute for Mathematics and Science at Penn State, Judith T. Witmer has managed various projects for the Pennsylvania Department of Education (PDE), including the Keystone Integrated Framework, Service Learning, and the Coalition of Essential Schools. She also has been an evaluator and researcher for the Penn State College of Medicine, Johns Hopkins Medical Center, Milton Hershey School, PDE, and many private institutions.

Dr. Witmer served two terms as President for the Advisory Board of the Pennsylvania Governor's Schools of Excellence and was a long-standing member of the Ethics Committee for Penn State's Milton S. Hershey Medical Center. She co-chaired the local fund-raising committee for building a new town library, which exceeded goal; chaired the 50th Anniversary celebration of Lower Dauphin High School, a year-long program culminating in four major events in a final 30-hour grand finale; and currently is serving as committee chair and editor of the commemorative publication for the Bicenquinquagennial Celebration of Hummelstown.

In addition to the number of books she has written, Judith Witmer has published numerous articles in professional journals, a cover feature in *Penn State Medicine*, newspaper columns, monographs, national speeches, book reviews, and a play. Her forthcoming book, *Growing Up Silent in the 1950s* is a social history, answering the question "Who are the Silent Generation and why were they silent?" Enlivening the historical framework are personal reflections by members of the Silent Generation through diaries, scrapbooks, interviews, memoirs, and personal reflections.

Acknowledgements

Designer and Layout Editor, **Elizabeth Nan Thompson Edmunds,** whose critical eye and clear understanding of this time in history led to the presentation of *All the Gentlemen Callers* in a skillful and fitting context.

Mrs. William Culbertson, whose husband was a friend of John I. Ditz who shared an interest in stock cars and aircraft.

Mr. William E. Culbertson, current owner of Cramer Marina, which had been the Cramer-Barstow Airport.

Mary Lea Lucas, Executive Director of the Clarion Historical Society, who shared information about the Sutton-Ditz House in a private tour of the facility.

Connie Smail, a Clarion native who took us on a walking tour and escorted us to the Airport which led to meeting Mr. William E. Culbertson.

Sara Frank Swartout, my high school classmate from Curwensville, who most kindly helped in connecting me with useful information about Clarion and its history.

Dedication

To All the Gentlemen Callers of every era who expressed their love and devotion through letters, to all the Belles who received and treasured them, and to a gentler time of handwritten letters and mail that was delivered twice daily.

All the Gentlemen Callers:
Letters Found in a 1920's Steamer Trunk

ISBN 978-0-9837768-1-9

Published in the United States by Yesteryear Publishing.

Books are available at **www.amazon.com** as well as through the publisher:

Yesteryear Publishing
P.O. Box 311
Hummelstown, PA 17036
www.yesteryearpublishing.com

yesteryearpublishing@gmail.com

(717) 566-8655

All the Gentlemen Callers is a collection of love letters and cards sent to Miss Jessie Beverly Pifer during the Roaring Twenties and the Great Depression. They are a tribute both to the receiver and to the writers who express the daily happenings in their lives, the effect of the historical time in which they lived and, most of all, their devotion to the beautiful, independent Miss Pifer, belle of the Class of 1924.

The letters and cards that appear here are authentic and the author has visited and/or researched most of the places mentioned herein. Samples of the actual handwritten letters are provided to emphasize the importance of writing letters which require the writer to reflect upon what is being expressed. As Roger Angell wrote in the January 2, 2012 issue of *The New Yorker*, "Losing the mixed pleasures of just arrived letters may not mean as much in the end as what we are missing by not writing them." Further, if we all should stop writing letters, how will our history be recorded by those who are a part of it and how will biographies ever be as accurate and personal as they have been, written in the unique handwriting of each letter writer?

List of Letters

All the Gentlemen Callers:
Letters Found in a 1920s Steamer Trunk

Jessie Beverly Pifer — dashing, independent, ever fashionable,
and always remembered as the beautiful, stylish, and vibrant
"Jebbie, Belle of the Class of 1924."

Shortly after completing the recent biography of my Aunt Jessie Pifer, I opened her steamer trunk (the high school graduation gift from her parents in 1924) to have a photograph taken of its fabric-lined interior to be used on the back cover of that book. When Jessie first moved to an assisted living facility I had not opened the drawers in the trunk because it felt intrusive. A few years later when circumstances compelled me to tell Jessie's story, I chose to keep the trunk closed and positioned so that the purple and gold decal in the shape of a pennant with the word "Clarion" emblazoned on it could best be viewed, serving as a daily reminder of Jessie's life and what had happened to her.

Expecting that the standing trunk would make a charming photograph, I set it upright and opened it, to best display its set of five drawers in graduated sizes on the right, integrated metal holding rods with custom-fitted wooden hangers of various shapes on the left, and its build-in cosmetic case on a swivel at the bottom. The photographer asked me to open the bottom drawer to give depth to the view of the trunk's interior and it was there that I found a dozen letters, tied with a white ribbon, that turned out to be from Jessie's high school and college girl friends. Under that small bundle I discovered a cache of more than 100 letters dating from 1924 to 1938, some tied together, others loose, but all addressed to "Jebbie" and all from her suitors during that period of her youth.

The letters, many beautiful in their own right because of the handwriting, now serve a variety of purposes—confirming information I had researched for Jessie's biography, clarifying other information, adding a first hand account of daily travails of life nearly a century ago, providing a parallel to modes of communication of then and now, displaying emotions familiar to all generations, and revealing the love and devotion of All the Gentlemen Callers.

To provide a setting for readers who do not know much about Jessie or who may not be familiar with the era of "Flaming Youth" followed by "The Great Depression," included here is an abbreviated historical background of the time and a glimpse into the life of "Jebbie" (the nicknamed given to her by the letter writer who first made her acquaintance in 1921[1]). The story is based on research, as well as Jessie's artifacts and family lore. This will provide the framework for the **Letters Found in a 1920s Steamer Trunk.**

The 1920s

At the beginning of the 1920s, the decade best known as "The Roaring Twenties," America was embracing the future, as new art modes were being developed in the form of movies and jazz, the musical play, and the skyscraper. American artists were enhancing musical appreciation for the masses with the phonograph and radio and through the launching of new journalism, notably *The New Yorker* and *The American Mercury*. Westinghouse opened the first American broadcasting station in Pittsburgh in 1922, transmitting regular radio programs the following year, and by 1924 coast-to-coast radio was available.

American literature was gaining more notice as the voice of contemporary issues and youth with the suave young F. Scott Fitzgerald (Princeton Class of 1917) portending the coming Jazz Age with his *This Side of Paradise* (1920), while Sinclair Lewis detailed small town life in America with *Main Street* (1921), followed in 1922 by *Babbitt*. Fitzgerald's *Tales of the Jazz Age* assured the place of "jazz age" as the most recognized descriptor for the 1920s.

On the stage, Eugene O'Neill's "The Emperor Jones" and "Beyond the Horizon" entranced a nation looking for a new identity following World War I. In the theatre, cynicism and brutal realism shocked many theatre-goers, particularly in 1924's "What Price Glory?" with its uncensored soldier jargon revealing the disillusionment of The Great War. On the screen Charlie Chaplin became "The Kid," and Mary Pickford (known as America's Sweetheart) played the lead in "Pollyanna," the story of a child with almost fatuous optimism.

In the early twentieth century the American marriage pattern was supporting the position of an ideal state of love *and* marriage, a situation beginning to be made possible by the spread of relatively efficient contraception (emphasis on "relatively"). People began to believe that sex, once freed from the threat of pregnancy, could be a source of mutual pleasure and that marriage could be defined as the necessary setting for the most pleasurable love. Ideally, love became the reason for sex and was promoted as meaning "being committed to marriage."

However, this ideal of "love with marriage" was shattered by the 1920s sexual revolution which demolished the familiar courtship system within the family structure, replacing the family-driven process with a dating structure built on a peer-driven system.[2] This peer system placed courtship into the public world and, instead of a young man "calling" on a young woman and visiting her in the family parlor under the scrutiny of their family, he would ask the young woman for a "date." If she agreed, he would "pick her up" at her home and the two of them would go off to a restaurant, theatre, tennis court, dance hall, or other public event.[3]

This practice of dating had the following results: (1) young couples went out on dates in public rather than getting to know one another quietly and over time on the front porch or parlor; (2) young people were no longer dependent on introductions through families; (3) a greatly liberalized definition of the kinds of physical interactions that were permissible between unmarried persons of the opposite sex occurred; (4) petting parties became a national craze;[4] (5) a young man was increasingly likely to have his first sexual encounter with a girlfriend rather than with a prostitute; and (6) marriage manuals (which included information regarding sexual matters for the married) became available for the uninitiated.

These marriage manuals, generally aimed at the middle class, began to acknowledge female sexuality, but continued to discuss sex in only the context of marriage. However, with the acceptance by the young of new practices, sexual rules changed. What had been the province of only those who were married became acceptable for those who became engaged.

Not surprising, it was on college campuses that many of the new conventions of post-World War I teenage sexual behavior were first established. It was college girls who first decided which sex acts a respectable girl could enjoy and which were illicit. It was college boys who first organized sex as a collective male activity and turned seductions into what they called "scores." And it was college couples who first turned "petting" (or its other euphemism "parking") into a routine activity. However, while this college youth culture was considered "liberating," females still were not liberated from the continuing double standard.[5]

Most young women of some privilege found themselves in a whirlpool of change like nothing before or since. Behind them was a stable family and secure childhood, one in which they did not have to leave school, as many of their less privileged classmates had done, in order to help support their families. They also were part of the first generation in which half of them would complete high school. In addition, they had personal freedom far beyond what previous generations of women had enjoyed, and most of their families were not pressing to arrange a marriage or to even suggest they should "find a husband."

Ahead of them was freedom to attend college and live away from home while attending classes, followed by a job to give them a measure of financial independence. Perhaps most importantly, they had the opportunity to choose marriage or remain single and support themselves. In this period that Studs Terkel called "a euphoric time,"[6] these lucky few thought they had most everything they could possibly want.

For the most part, young women who chose to work during the 1920s would be expected to remain living at home, for single women did not ever live alone. To flounce off into a boarding house or an apartment, even with a roommate, would have been unheard of. By the end of the decade, however, in areas where small kitchenette apartments were available, some single women throughout the country began to move out of their homesteads. There was also the possibility of purchasing an automobile which would provide a modicum of freedom.

Yet for all the opportunities opening for young women, the other side of that freedom was that for the first time in modern history, most life choices were more difficult with no clear expected behaviors. With the revolution in morals and manners, single women suddenly found themselves having to decide whether to remain quiet and modest or vocal and "smart." While almost every young woman wanted to be thought of as smart, not all of them were sure they wanted to follow the expectations that went with being viewed as sophisticated, such as using cigarettes, liquor, and strong language.

Social dancing, barely mentioned in the press before 1900, also had a great effect on the new dating code as it gained great popularity after a "dance palace" opened in New York City in 1911. The concept of a place specifically designated for mixed dancing greatly appealed to the young, and the idea spread rapidly. A place to go to dance opened a whole new world, one in which music seemed to encourage easy and spontaneous contact between members of the opposite sex. Dancing in these halls was less formalized than dances organized by social clubs so that almost anyone could get on the floor without knowing even the rudiments of ballroom dancing. This was a great relief to those who were ready to break away from the high school-approved formal waltz, two-step, and quadrille.

Where dating provided a way to manage the social demands of the new peer society, dancing provided the means by which to cultivate heretofore unheard of physical closeness. It wasn't long before dancing was established as a commercial leisure activity and regarded as a social action that emphasized romantic relationships.[7] While critics claimed that public dance halls fostered casualness between partners, permitted greater options in holding partners, and symbolized the high value placed on mutual heterosexual intimacy and attraction,[8] others believed that dancing laid a positive foundation for more candor between the sexes.

Nonetheless, this frankness was criticized for being more of an invitation for physical closeness and less of an encouragement for the face-to-face and heart-to-heart talking that had occurred in earlier courtships. Those who believed that the earlier practice of sharing confidences had been important as a measure of intimacy between engaged men and women saw the new style of courtship as inhibiting emotional directness.[9] It has been suggested that the physical openness of dancing was one factor in the rapid spread of petting among young people, a practice that was to proliferate in the next few decades.

Despite what some observers saw as obvious risks, high schools soon began offering school dances as a kind of "structured" sociability. This sanction by the schools made it more difficult for many parents to say "no" to dancing. The Lynds, in particular, said that school dances should not be discouraged because they offered "an exceptional opportunity for training."[10]

Movies had a similar effect on socializing and lessening of parental control since a darkened theatre provided accompanying music (capable of being suggestive in various ways) and close theatre seating (setting the tone of privacy and intimacy). Further, the movie screen provided examples of love at first, second, and third sight; of winning another's love; and of a successful culmination of this love through marriage and otherwise. For impressionable, willing-to-learn youth, the films also provided explicit content for sexual fantasies and instruction in lovemaking techniques.[11] Considering that between 1921 and 1930 average weekly movie attendance increased rapidly and a weekly visit to the movies would be typical for young unmarried persons, it isn't hard to imagine how social and personal interaction changed.

Many parents did not discourage movie attendance because they believed the movie studios' own claims that they were showing high school culture as innocent, light-hearted, and fun. Other adults, however, continued to maintain that youth were watching movies that presented examples of how to challenge parental authority. Also, it is highly likely that other young people across America were pulling the same stunt that a group of high school students in Curwensville did, giggling among themselves the evening they all had convinced their parents that it would be "good for them" to see Cecil B. DeMille's "The Ten Commandments." The high schoolers had heard the film's attraction was not its Biblical accuracy but rather its spectacular staging and revealing costumes, and they wanted to see this for themselves.[12]

Of high interest to the general public were "the talkies"—the single most technological advance in the theatre industry. The first talking picture was Al Jolson in "The Jazz Singer," but DeMille's "King of Kings" was said to be the movie with the most spectacular effects since "The Ten Commandments." With the addition of sound, movies soon rose to the position of a vast industry and movies soon drew millions of people into the theatres every twenty-four hours, with the average movie-goer attending "the pictures" more than once a week.

In addition to expanding their knowledge about life by watching the movies, young women also were being manipulated by advertisers into buying the products that were used in the film stories. Soon items such as silk stockings, high-heeled shoes, permanent waves, and one-piece bathing suits—seen in both the movies and in newspaper and magazine ads—quickly became standard with young women everywhere. The emerging fashion industry made it easier for social classes to resemble one another, and young purchasers began to believe in the American dream of equal opportunity—or at least equal exhibition—for all.

Styles in clothing were changing drastically and by the middle of the decade the amount of fabric in a woman's outfit had decreased to half of what it had been at the beginning of the decade. Styles had gone from amply cut ankle-length dresses over such underpinnings as corset covers, envelope chemises, and petticoats to dresses designed to make the wearer look as pencil-slim as possible, all of these knee-length over silk or artificial silk undergarments. It was with these fashions that girls' bodies became increasingly "public." Thus, girls' attention to dieting and preoccupation with body shape began in earnest for the first time in history when advertising, advice columns, and stories in magazines equated thinness with popularity, fun, and the all-important dating.

Across the country adults watched as "flaming youth" was having its fling. By mid-decade skirts were becoming shorter and women were striving for the first time to create a boyish figure by dropping the waistline of their dresses to the hips. Together with a loose and flopping coat and unbuttoned galoshes, this silhouette suggested the description "flapper,"[13] the term that identified stylish young women of the period. Self-styled flappers displayed rolled down stockings, knee-length skirts and bobbed hair.[14] Some of them, with cigarettes dangling from reddened lips, further enjoyed shocking their elders by dancing the Charleston and the Black Bottom, and engaging in other activities termed as "inventions of the devil."

As expected, adults were dumb-struck at the close embraces of the modern dances, the more open displays of "touching the opposite sex," and the promiscuous physical contact of "necking."[15] Many parents were horrified at what they viewed as indecorous parties and were appalled at the extent of gate crashing, an action unheard of by previous generations. Further, adults recoiled in stunned surprise at the open dialogue about sex among these young adults and some questioned if the younger generation had gone mad.

> *Hon, I'd just love you most to death. I'd like to throw a real necking party with just us two as participants. I would just hold you so tightly and I'd kiss you until you'd plead for mercy.*
>
> Unsigned Letter, 1928

In Curwensville, however, Jessie Pifer and her pals could only yearn for such sophistication, doing their best to appear to be "savvy," a favorite word of the high school juniors who had begun to connect English words with the French they were struggling to learn in Mr. Zetler's class, wishing it to add some "pep" (another new slang word just making its way into the popular culture) to their mundane existence.

What those in small towns didn't realize, of course, is that these youngsters were at best only mildly imitating their more daring counterparts in the cities and in college towns. For example, most people in small towns would not have known a speakeasy if they had fallen into it. While they pretended they knew where speakeasies could be found—and assumed people frequented them— they did not personally know anyone who had ever set foot in one.

In the fall of 1920 Jessie Beverly Pifer felt a sense of momentousness in entering high school. In a building with 20 teachers and nearly five hundred students, 36 of those were members of the Freshman Class, a number that, by graduation, would be reduced by one-third.

The second week of school a freshman class meeting was held, at which time the frosh were to select class colors and a motto and to elect class officers. However, it took them three class meetings to come to an agreement and elect one of the boys as class president and to choose their class colors of purple and gold, and a motto of *Veni! Vidi! Vici!*, adding its translation for those who might need it. Yellow roses won out over purple iris on the point that irises weren't elegant enough.

7

Outgoing and gregarious, with a great many friends, Jessie was honing a style that would remain with her. One of those friends and Jessie purchased and actually *used* Tangee lipstick, nearly a decade before *The Ladies Home Journal* agreed to advertisements for the product. Jessie saw nothing wrong with using the lipstick, despite warnings from her father that explicitly forbade the use of make-up for any of his daughters.

As sophomores Jessie and her friends were filled with their own self-importance. Jessie had already bobbed her hair, much to the dismay of her mother, and her parents were concerned that she was becoming far too outspoken and independent. Her mother did not like this "attitude" of Jessie, and, like most parents, believed her daughter was being negatively influenced by her friends.

From an early age Jessie never let work get in the way of having a good time. She was very popular and wherever the fun was, Jessie was in the center of it. Nothing was more important to Jessie and her crowd than to be thought "smart," a word that in the 1920s took on the connotation "fashionable" after the American fashion world assumed the term from the French.

With many new machines at this time freeing more people from the drudgery of routine chores, the growth of leisure time led to a vast increase in sports, especially in spectator sports like baseball, football, basketball, and hockey. Smaller colleges began to expand interscholastic competition and college football became more popular with the general public, creating a burgeoning cult of the Saturday afternoon college football scene.

Golf and tennis, which at the turn of the century had been regarded by the public as games of the idle rich, also became popular in the 1920s. Young people found playing tennis an acceptable form of recreation—as well as a convenient way to spend time with friends. Because it was a relatively safe activity and one that attracted the youth in groups, parents were generally willing to agree to their maturing children's requests to "go to the tennis courts."

Fashions began to reflect this easy style and panache of the carefree life of the collegian and, even at a young age, Jessie longed for a raccoon coat. Buying one was entirely out of the question, but she counted the days until she might earn her own money enough to buy a possum coat and hope that no one would notice the difference.

Another trend that influenced some high schools was the imitation of secret societies, patterned on those of some college students or young wealthy women of college age. The main focus of these societies, such as "the Zulus" fictionalized by Upton Sinclair in his novel *Oil*, was exclusivity of a certain social class in which its members lived by a strict social code of behavior, much of it clandestine.[16] This was all a part of youth becoming more independent. The criteria of acceptability into the societies were attributes of manner, dress, and style. These, of course, were related to family background, economic position, and prep-school training, but could also be cultivated.[17]

In the fall of 1922 Jessie won the lead role in the town production of the musical comedy "Kathleen." She later carefully placed in her senior memory book the promotional green cardboard cloverleaf which advertised the show to the public as being presented on December 14, 1922. It was with this event that the names of young men began to appear in writing in her mementoes. Jessie noted that "Terry [McGovern] came to see me perform Kathleen" and that she had "just started to go with [Winfield] Sykes."[18] Thus, at age seventeen began what would become a long procession of gentleman callers.

While very likely every male in her class had a crush on Jessie, she counted Joe Errigo as her best friend, although they didn't date. She mentions going to two social events with John Wright and the names of others, including Clifford Kelley, Orville Hipps, Gunnard Olson, and Dave McKinley '23 (later head of the College of Business at Penn State who also was a favorite beau of Jessie's friend Mary Alice Thompson), appear in Jessie's *Girl Graduate* memory book.

Francis X. "Terry" McGovern was Jessie's first beau outside of her own high school acquaintances and he became her most faithful—and persistent—suitor. His letters account for about a quarter of those discovered in the trunk and in her writing desk. Jessie had first met Terry in the summer of 1921. A later letter from him (March 18, 1925) suggests that they had met when Jessie was visiting relatives in Coalport, which was Terry's home until his family moved to Emporium in the fall of 1923. Terry's relationship with Jessie ran the range from avuncular good friend to lover to confidante, with "being in love with her" always the underlying theme.

On the other hand, **Winfield Sykes** was her first serious "fella" in high school, although there were no letters found in the trunk from him. While his name appears in some of Jessie's own remembrances and there is a photograph of him, there is nothing to validate the extent of their involvement. He likely is the brother of Irene Sykes, a friend of Jessie's in Curwensville, and he also may have attended Clarion Normal School.

From all indications Jessie's junior year of high school was a very eventful one for the time. According to the 1923 yearbook describing the Junior Class History, "We entertained the Seniors at Viewpoint and everyone enjoyed that trip. We also enjoyed a trip to Clearfield. This proved quite an exciting time for all. Next a social was held at the Grange Hall and one at the Moose Hall."[19] A milestone for Jessie was being given permission by her parents to occasionally stop after school at Jimmy's Sweet Shoppe. Jimmy's was the place where the young people gathered to talk and pool their resources if only to share an ice cream soda.

The Sweet Shoppe was the closest thing to a "hang-out" that the young people had, although they usually just stopped by for a drink or ice cream, as few of their parents allowed them to linger.

Winfield Sykes

This was also the year of a new friendship for Jessie with the Thompson family who had moved across the street from the Pifers. Mary Alice Thompson, officially a junior, had earned enough credits to join the graduating class of 1923, but decided to remain at home for a year and to take two additional courses with the class of 1924. (Such a practice was routine in a time when only a few years earlier high school was a three-year program—freshman, junior, and senior years. and students easily moved between graduating classes, depending upon how many credits they had earned.)

Jessie, Mary Alice, and Marjorie Wall (Jessie's long-standing pal as well as Mary Alice's cousin) became fast friends. All living on Thompson Street, it was easy for Jessie to ask permission to visit friends whose front porches could be kept in sight of her parents. When her father was home, he often told Jessie she could go only to Mary Alice's front porch, but because Mary Alice's father didn't like the young people gathering on his front porch, Jessie had an acceptable explanation for her father to be permitted to join the young people who congregated on the back porch, blessedly obscured from Papa's sight line.

Here on warm summer nights could be heard talking, laughing, and, when Harold Smith brought his ukulele, occasionally singing. Jessie's voice could often be heard above the others, and neighborhood families sitting on their porches would stop their conversation to listen.

Mary Alice opened opportunities for Jessie to meet even more young people since the Thompsons had lived in Clearfield and, before that, in Bellefonte. In the following years there would be many "double dates" with Mary Alice.

At eighteen, "Jebbie" (a variation of "J.B.," coined by Terry McGovern for Jessie Beverly), as she was called by her friends, was what both boys and girls called "a looker." Slender and tall, she also boasted a long narrow waist. True to the style of the time, Jessie's high school graduation portrait shows a proper, but slightly pouting, beauty with a styled bob, double-dropped pearl earrings, a fine wool dress trimmed with marabou and, as a finishing touch, a long strand of pearls.

Jessie liked "nice things," especially clothing and accessories. Unfortunately there was no way to acquire these, so she quickly learned to talk a good game so that friends would never suspect the Pifers were not too far from the designation of genteel poverty. On one particular occasion, a visiting friend of Jessie's—Jessie seemed to have an endless stream of friends, both male and female— found herself ready to leave as a rain shower began. Not to be abashed or deterred by fact that the Pifer family did not own an umbrella, Jessie, with great poise, asked of the household, "Where is the pearl-handled one?" Fortunately, the rain abated, and there was no need for embarrassment at not being able to offer the use of an umbrella, a non-existent pearl-handled one notwithstanding.

In the fall of 1923 one of the first things the Class of 1924 did was to hang the class pennant in the senior homeroom. Looking back, a member of the Class of 1924 mused, "You would have thought we were the French who had conquered England." This "hanging of the colors" signaled an esprit de corps that had been missing in their class to date. The members had squabbled among themselves over everything from the class colors and motto to who would be photographed in the yearbook.

As to calling cards, each class member could choose his or her own style. Jessie repeated the exercise she had first attempted as a freshman and tried out every version of her name, wishing her middle name were more reminiscent of grander heritage, something like the name of her cousin: *Catherine Princetta Shields.* Without that, the best she could do, she decided, was to use the Gothic font style which at least looked significantly important. Throughout her lifetime she kept the metal engraving plate in its original envelope ready to mail to Quayle & Son, Inc. should she ever choose to order additional cards.

Even in a small town and with a senior class of only 27 members, Jessie and her friends found ways to have fun. On October 31, 1923 the seniors held a Halloween Social in the American Legion rooms where the Ladies Auxiliary served as chaperones. All members of the class were masked and in costume. Dancing, fortune telling, and refreshments were features of the evening.

In January the yearbook process began. Every member of the class had an assigned position, if only in name, and none had any idea of how to publish a yearbook. Jessie, not particularly interested in the structure a publication required, was satisfied to be one of two "Wise and Otherwise Editors," responsible for only two pages, one of jokes and the other a listing of all seniors, of what they were fond, future occupation, and nickname.

In late January Jessie requested a college catalogue from Clarion State Normal School. This she frequently carried with her, as if to announce that she soon would be a coed. She wasn't really serious about becoming a full-time student because there was no money for full-time enrollment and working one's way through college was not an option for females. Further, she wasn't convinced that she wanted to spend four years studying. What did attract her, however, was the *idea* of college, as she pored over the catalogue, dreaming of dormitories and socials, fraternities and football games, pennants, friends, and suitors.

On Monday, February 12, 1924, the CHS Senior Class embarked on a class sleigh ride. Waving to the underclassmen who were readying for their first class period, the Class of 1924 attached their class pennant to the rear of the large sleigh, and vied for the best seats, preferably near a member of the opposite sex. Jessie, in her usual manner, had promised at least half a dozen classmates that she would sit with them, and when she arrived all were clamoring for her favor. "Here, Jebbie, I saved you a seat." "Jess, I brought a warm sleigh blanket for us." "Jessie Beverly, remember, you promised you would sit with me."

Acknowledging none of their pleas, Jessie instead turned to Joe Errigo and asked, "Can someone help me climb in?" In a flash she was surrounded by many male arms very willing to oblige. Jessie wore a smart pair of boots, impracticably trimmed with ruching sewn to resemble fur. These were a Christmas present from Mama, who knew such boots were not a sensible choice for long wear, but that Jessie had her heart set on something fashionable. Jessie's coat was wool, rather than the raccoon she longed for, but she had begged her married sister Ruby to borrow her brightly colored muffler, promising to return it by mail immediately after the excursion.

Jessie was as noticeably chic as anyone in a small town in 1924 could be. "Very Vo-goo," said Clifford Kelly, complimenting Jessie and laughing at the way the entire French class liked to mispronounce French words such as "vogue." "And chick, chick, chic!" added Kay Wrigley. By now all were merry and full of themselves, anticipating the scene they would make as they traveled down the highway to Clearfield, seven miles distance, to their destination, the center of town where the high school was located. Nearly twenty of them were crowded in the sleigh intended for sixteen, but no one complained. They sang and shouted cheers for most of the way, drawing attention to themselves, which was, of course, their intention.

The entourage arrived at Clearfield High School around ten o'clock, creating, as they had planned and later reported, "a sensation."[20] They disembarked with practiced nonchalance, fully aware that the students in the high school building were standing at the windows watching them. The sleigh riders then sauntered merrily for half a block to Murphy's Pig and Whistle Shop, a sweet shop where they had hot chocolate, and more so, deliciously enjoyed the display they were creating. They returned to their sleigh an hour or so later and, exhilarated, were ready for the return trip. No one complained of the cold, and by the time they were halfway home, most of the class were snuggled together, fully expecting never to forget this great adventure.

Around three o'clock the sleigh made the turn into Curwensville where the road took a steep incline. The horses were tiring, and Gunnard Olson suggested the class walk the rest of the way. Jessie said, "But it's cold." What she meant was that she didn't want to ruin her new boots. Joe, disentangling himself from her embrace, gallantly suggested that the boys walk alongside the sleigh and let the girls remain seated. That suggestion was appealing and even more attention-getting for their arrival at the high school. When Jessie suggested they all sing the Alma Mater, with the girls quartette taking the verses and all joining the chorus, the vote was unanimous. Indeed, "the home town welcomed us back again."[21]

Shortly after this event an Atwater Kent radio was delivered to the Pifer home where it was placed in the front room beside the front window, everyone's favorite vantage point for viewing events occurring in the center of town. While the Pifer house was not large enough for young people to congregate and listen to the radio, there were other homes of a size where they could gather in the parlor while the parents kept close watch from an adjoining sitting room. However, the only way all of them could hear the music on the radio was to place the headset in a wash tub so that the sound reverberated enough for more than one person to hear.

True, the sound was a bit "tinny," but Jessie loved to dance and, when there were orchestras "broadcast live from New York," she was the first on her feet. Jessie had a knack for learning the latest dances, usually from observation of the college crowd (a handful at best) who occasionally joined the high school group at their informal get-togethers.

Cast of Miss Somebody Else

March afternoons and evenings were filled with rehearsals for the senior class play, cast entirely from the class membership and including 15 speaking roles. Directed by the high school faculty, "Miss Somebody Else," a comedy in four acts, was presented by the Senior Class at the Opera House on Friday evening, March 21. Jessie's appearance in the cast photograph is strikingly exotic, and, even three-quarters of a century later, her perfect oval face and fine features are clearly evident, her hair stylishly designed with a large "spit curl" centered on her forehead.

Immediately following the play, a Senior Class Dance was held at the Legion room. Jessie chose to wear her costume from the play and made even more than her usual dramatic entrance.

Near the end of April, the 1924 yearbooks were delivered. And on arrival, there was no doubt that this was "the best yearbook ever" (relatively speaking since this was only the third year in Curwensville for a yearbook). Formal graduation announcements were readied and mailed out in mid-May. Jessie was surprised and pleased to recognize the seal heading the announcement as being the embossed design of their class ring.[22] The design notwithstanding, like most of her classmates she had ordered more announcements than she could use, forgetting that her mother had cautioned her not to send to anyone who would think she was soliciting gifts.

On May 31 Jessie received her first graduation gift, *The Girl Graduate*: *Her Own Book*.[23] The book was designed as a keepsake with pages designated for memorabilia surrounding graduation. Pleased with the gift, as she was a collector (but not a cataloguer) of souvenirs, Jessie carefully entered the date she received the book, along with the class flower, colors, and motto; names of teachers; and class officers. Jessie took care to get the autograph of every member of her class. More in typical Jessie fashion, however, items are pasted pell-mell throughout the book, with clippings, invitations, paper napkins from special restaurants, programs from plays, and train ticket stubs glued in without written dates and in no sequential order.

While it is likely that she received additional gifts, under the entry for "Gifts" Jessie has listed only two items, a wardrobe trunk and a watch, both of which are likely to have come from her parents. Her watch, a gold Hamilton, was a treasured possession as wrist watches were not common, especially for persons of little means. The trunk, while expensive, was a necessity, since Jessie would need it when she left for Clarion State Normal School in June.

Baccalaureate Services were held in the Presbyterian Church and once the class began its solemn processional, Jessie's notation in her graduation book under *Baccalaureate Sermon* was typically Jessie: "Everybody feeling great. All seniors present but one. Date with John Wright."

Commencement Exercises were held June 3 in the Strand Theatre. By this time, walking in a procession seemed natural and Jessie was looking forward to the main event, the theatre sure to be filled with parents and friends. Led by the class officers, the seniors entered to the strains of "Unfinished Symphony" by Shubert.

Immediately following the ceremony, without even looking at their final report cards, the graduates hurried to the event which marked them as adults—the Annual Alumni Banquet, held immediately following Commencement. The final event to mark the close of the 1924 school year was the Annual Alumni Public School Picnic, held the following day at Irvin Park.

Ahead of her, Jessie had college and freedom to live away from home while attending classes; a job to give her a measure of financial independence; and the opportunity, in time, to choose marriage or remain single. Jessie believed she had most everything she could want and would be holding her destiny in her own hands.

The increasing democratization of America led to expanded educational opportunities, adding to the freedom young people began to experience. "Co-ed" education provided situations in which young men and women learned to be more comfortable in one another's company, and women became more confident of not only their academic ability, but also of their independent status.

Because of the proximity in which young people found themselves, both in high school and college, they became more open in displaying their new-found self-governance. Further, adults recoiled in shocked surprise at the free conversation about sex. Many wondered if the younger generation was obsessed by the subject since its members devoured the current confession magazines, sex-filled movies …

Haven't even seen many movies. "Wings" is the best movie in years. Not much plot but heavy on the photography and how![24] "Underworld" is also an excellent movie.[25] Saw it twice.

—John Ditz, February 18, 1928

Saw 5 movies last week. "Dressed to Kill"[26] and Charlie Chaplain in "The Circus"[27] were about the best. Saw one called "The Showdown"[28] last night. It was fairly good.

—John Ditz, March 28, 1928

Just got back from a bus ride. Went to pass the time. Movies last night and again this afternoon. Heard Waring's Pennsylvanians.[29]

—John Ditz, April 5, 1928

…and passionate books.

Been spending most of my spare time reading books from a circulating library. Some I can recommend are

"The Madonna of the Sleeping Cars"

"The Marriage Bed" (very good in spite of the title)

"The Circus Parade" (Dandy)

"Gas—Drive In" (Good, light love story)

Just started reading "Oil" by Upton Sinclair and it promises to be good.

—John Ditz, February 28, 1928

Managed by accident to get hold of one mean, passionate book called "Dream of a Woman."

You would like it, but I don't know where I could get a copy for you to read.

—John Ditz, March 28, 1928

Read several good books. "He Knew Women," a novel; and a biography of Disraeli.

—John Ditz, May 18, 1928

Silk stockings, high-heeled shoes, permanent waves, and one-piece bathing suits—all were becoming standard with young women everywhere, leading them to feel at one with all economic classes. An emerging industry in "fashion" was making it easier for social classes to resemble one another, and even women began to believe in the American dream of equal opportunity for all.

Jessie's idea of equal opportunity was, for the present, limited to attending college and being able to do what other young people (both male and female) were doing. She probably didn't fully

Jebbie (far left) and friends

appreciate the additional freedom afforded her in being permitted to enroll in Clarion—a state-supported school, rather than the conservative Grove City College her two older sisters had attended. Like most young people, beginning with her generation, she took all privileges for granted. All she consciously realized was that she was headed to college.

None of the detailed history, geography, or organizational structure of Clarion State Normal School (CSNS) explained in the catalogue mattered to Jessie Beverly Pifer, member of the Freshman Class at CSNS in the summer of 1924. To Jessie and the many others attending Summer School for teachers, what was important was that they were, with all that implied, "college students."

Clarion likely would have sent each perspective student a description of the dormitory room, typical of the time, "Each room contains a chiffonier, one straight chair, one rocking chair for each girl and then a table and bookcase for both…. In making your plans for furnishing your rooms do not forget a couch cover, sofa pillows, pictures and table light if preferred. If assigned to McAllister Hall furnish curtains since the closets have no doors. Napkin rings are desirable."[30]

Jessie spent weeks packing her wardrobe trunk long before graduation and had been saving tissue paper for padding her clothes at least since Christmas. Of course, not all of it had been saved in one locale; rather, there were sheets and pieces of sheets of tissue paper in the upstairs hall cabinets, in the attic, in the dining room sideboard, in a box under Jessie's bed, and even under the cushion of the easy chair in the dining room. She had read or heard from older friends that in packing, dresses should be filled with tissue paper as if they were being worn. By the time she had come to preparing the third dress, however, she lost patience, realizing that by using so much tissue paper not all of her even limited wardrobe would fit in the trunk.

After everything was packed the trunk was hauled by Mr. Korb, a local drayman, to the Pennsylvania Railroad passenger and freight station. There both trunk and Jessie stood, with ticket in hand, anticipating a great adventure. Jessie could hardly wait to board the train as she looked forward in eager anticipation for the first person to inquire of her destination.

At Clarion Jessie was met by a porter who transported the trunk the "half square" distance (as it was described in the college catalog) to the girls' dormitory. Clutching the Summer Session calendar in her hand, Jessie was filled with excitement and bravado. She knew no one, but her naturally gregarious personality soon assumed her "grande dame" hostess role in greeting all the later arrivals. By the end of the day most of the girls had arrived in the dormitory and friendships began to form immediately.

Following a get-acquainted luncheon the next day, a group of girls on Jessie's floor decided to explore the campus and the town. While too naïve to realize that the small town of Clarion was quite accustomed to having new college students, this novice band of co-eds tried to act as if they had always been part of the college scene. Their stopping to buy postcards at A.G. Corbett Drug Company and posing for photos, however, was a sure sign to everyone that they were freshmen. Congregated and giggling on the front steps of the County Courthouse, the girls were approached by a group of Clarion High School students, carrying their class pennant announcing "CHS 1925." One of the girls in the college group lived in Clarion and provided introductions.

As expected, Jessie immediately caught the eye of the handsome president of the Clarion High School Class of 1925 and son of a prominent town family. **William "Bill" L. Fowler** was self-assured, a letterman in football, basketball, and track, and was about to lead his class for the third time as its chief officer. He was the first of many in Clarion who were smitten by Jessie Pifer. Bill remained one of her long-time favorites, one she would continue to date for several years to come and the one who loaned her his high school yearbook (which, characteristically, she forgot to return).

The following day after the exploration of Clarion and on her way back to the dormitory, Jessie was hailed by one of the other young men who had been with the local crowd the day before. "Hello!" he said. "I just happened to be running an errand and thought I might run into you. I'm John Ditz (pronounced "Deets"), in case you don't remember all our names from yesterday." "I remember," Jessie replied. "You are the one who has the car with the odd name." John laughed. "Would you like to go for a ride some day after class in that car?" Jessie said she would think about it, as she wasn't sure she knew him well enough to ride in his car.

Bill L. Fowler

John I. Ditz, Bill's best friend, was an honor student and basketball manager at Clarion High School. Affable, sincere, and good-looking, John was described in the *1925 Clarionette* as "the sheik of our class. His car, the Chalmers, is the envy of every boy, and it is the ambition of every girl to claim a ride." John's letters to Jebbie are second in number only to those of Terry McGovern.

John I. Ditz

Jessie's friends had always said to her, "Jessie, you certainly can pick them!" Here she hadn't been in town two days yet, and already the two most eligible boys in the senior class at Clarion High School were vying for her attention. Before the summer was over, Bill and John would have nearly come to blows over the affections of Jessie Pifer. After one particularly harsh argument, strong words were exchanged and John called Bill by a pejorative term. He immediately regretted it, as Bill and he had been best friends since childhood. Bill had walked away rather than allow their argument to become a fist fight they both would greatly regret.

Clarion Normal School Summer Class 1924 (left half of the panoramic photo)

John, not wanting to break their friendship, wrote a hasty note of apology on the back of an order sheet from the Clarion Dry Cleaning Company and sent it to Bill through a mutual friend. Bill later gave the note to Jessie:

Dear Bill,

Please forgive me for calling you that, not that I want to apologize for taking the liberty to do so.

John Ditz

Back at the dormitory after her chance meeting with John Ditz, Jessie remembered she had promised to send a post card to her mother to tell her she had arrived safely and was settled in her room. Unabashed at her own forgetfulness, she wrote a quick note and set the card aside to mail the next day. There wasn't time to go to the post office, if she wanted to be fully prepared for the social planned for that evening. Having noted months ago that the CSNS colors of purple and gold were the same as her own class colors, she had packed a borrowed scarf in those colors. For her first college social, Jessie donned an unadorned black dress, knotted the scarf around her neck, and strutted down the hall, confident that she would be an attention-getter. She was right.

The following day, a photograph of the class was taken. That photo remains yet today, details still crisp, revealing a group of eager young people standing at the launching of their adult life.

The bon mot was her métier. She had a sharp eye and ear for current words, especially for slang, and she enjoyed watching people's reactions to her use of the language. With a keen intellect, she found her quips kept her in center stage. "Neat" is one of the many slang terms she introduced to her friends who had known the word only as meaning "tidy."

Clarion Normal School Summer Class 1924 (right half of the panoramic photo)

The bon mot was Jessie's métier. She had a sharp eye and ear for current words, especially for slang, and she enjoyed watching people's reactions to her use of the language. With a keen intellect, she found her quips kept her in center stage. "Neat" is one of the many slang terms she introduced to her friends who had known the word only as meaning "tidy."

Even though the summer program at Clarion was intended to be compressed and intense, Jessie and her friends had many good times, some recorded through mementos and annotations in her *Girl Graduate* memory book, and others only implied. Jessie, like countless others before and since, kept such souvenirs as programs, paper napkins or match covers, writing on them the date of the event.

Born for the life of a fun-loving coed, Jessie enjoyed being a trend setter, even though it was on a small college campus, little known except by those in the surrounding counties. Like most who attended Clarion State, Jessie had a very limited wardrobe. Unlike most of her contemporaries, however, she had a flair for accessories, both bought and found objects. While Jessie could not sew anything more than a bouquet of fabric flowers onto a belt, she made up for this lack of skill by ingenuity. If a piece of costume jewelry broke she would take the remaining part and glue it on a hat or belt or coat. And she also was known to simply wear the jewelry piece, missing stones or not.

The first of the many cards and letters later found in Jessie's trunk arrived on July 9, 1924, her nineteenth birthday, a date Terry McGovern never forgot in his diligence and regard for Jessie.

Jessie was popular with everyone, as the *Girl Graduate* book she had taken with her to Clarion reveals. Among the many who wrote their names in the autograph section of the memory book that first summer are Winfield Sykes and Bill Fowler.

Clarion provided many activities and events for its Summer Term students. Jessie took full advantage of these offerings, immersing herself in all cultural events and leading a very full social life, both on campus and off.

Not all of the activities in which she likely participated are confirmed; however, near the end of the term Jessie attended the Second Annual Recital by Nathan Aaron, Violinist. This recital evidently was one of campus prominence, as it boasted its own printed program, complete with program notes,[31] an event special enough to find itself memorialized in Jessie's *Girl Graduate* book.

One Friday, Joe Errigo, high school classmate and close friend, and Jim Holden, drove from Curwensville to Clarion for a double date with Jessie and her roommate. Such a visit created quite a stir in the dormitory, as Jessie intended to ride back to Curwensville, unchaperoned, late at night with the two young men, to spend the week-end at home. It was nearly a scandal, as Jessie

did not have written permission from her parents. When she returned to the dormitory around ten o'clock after the double date at the movies and realized that she might forfeit her entire summer's work and be expelled for leaving with these two friends, she decided the trip home was not worth the risk. As Jessie's best pal and protector since childhood, Joe agreed with her that it would be better for her to stay on campus.

This interruption of plans did not, however, deter her the following week from going home by train to attend a swimming party, as well as the Clearfield County Annual Picnic the following day. She returned to Clarion on the evening train to be present for a review for exams.

Opening her first Teacher's Contract made Jessie feel very grown up, as she read she was being assigned to "teach in Fairview school house for the term of 8 months, at a compensation of $85. per school month, to be paid monthly."[32] As part of her contract, Jessie would board at the homes of various members of the school board, depending upon who had a room for the "school ma'm."

Jessie was nineteen years of age and weighed 110 pounds when she began her first year of teaching, a career that would continue for forty-five years. Her school was a one-room, barn-like building "in the middle of nowhere," as she described it to her friends. There was no paved road, as the school was perched on a knoll near the edge of a farmer's field. The only access was to follow the path that had been worn into the field for the past thirty years. The clay-like ground was always either a sea of mud because of rain or dusty from lack of it. Two small buildings were located near the school house, one for coal and the other an outhouse. A tiny porch served as the entrance to the school and on top of the structure was a bell whose rope hung down just inside the door.

Jessie needed to muster all of her authority, theatrical skills, and bluffing techniques to keep order day after day, especially since some of the students were taller (and, she suspected, older) than she was. She was the sole adult in charge of 35 children of various ages and varying abilities. Most of them were respectful of her position, and all knew that if they were disciplined in school, they would face additional punishment at home. Jessie began developing what her family later would call her "teacher tone," a kind of authoritative assurance. By the end of October, there was no doubt just who was in charge: Miss Pifer had arrived.

For the first time Jessie had a bit of money of her own. After contributing $30 a month to the household, she still had money enough to buy some of the clothes she had wanted. Disappointingly, however, there was not enough *yet* to buy the raccoon coat for which she yearned.

The weeks were often long for Jessie as she moved from one school director's home to another during the course of the year. She prepared her lessons either in the evenings or after school, but because she didn't sew, sometimes the evenings were interminably slow in passing. She could spend only so much time preparing art projects for the students, and she wearied of trying to avoid prying questions from the school director or his wife.

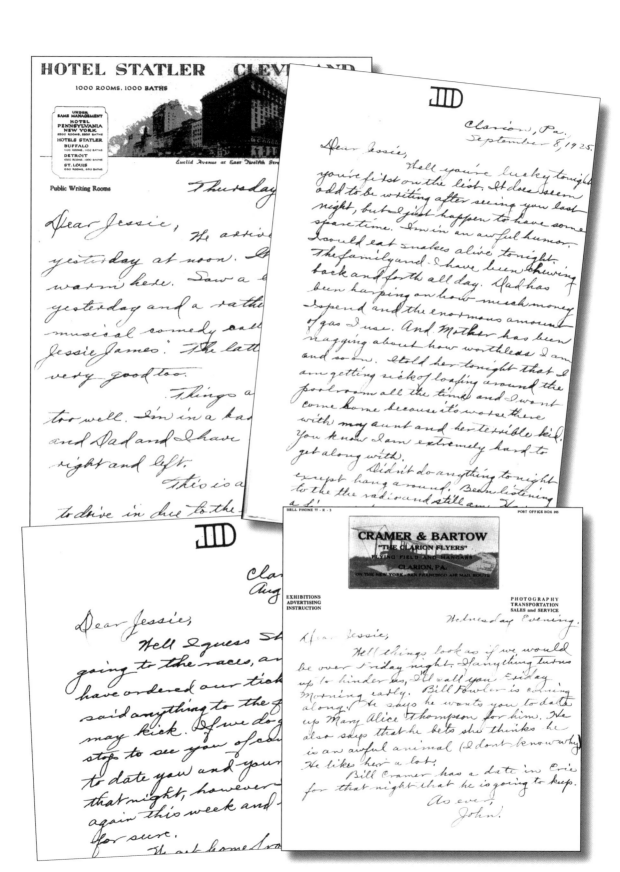

HOTEL STATLER CLEVELAND
1000 ROOMS, 1000 BATHS

UNDER SAME MANAGEMENT
HOTEL PENNSYLVANIA NEW YORK
2200 ROOMS, 2200 BATHS
HOTELS STATLER
BUFFALO
DETROIT
ST. LOUIS

Euclid Avenue at East Twelfth Street

Public Writing Rooms

Thursday

Dear Jessie,

We arrived
yesterday at noon.
warm here. Saw a
yesterday and a rather
musical comedy call
Jessie James". The latt
very good too.

Things a
too well. I'm in a bad
and Dad and I have
right and left.

This is a
to drive in due to the

Clarion, Pa.,
September 8, 1925.

Dear Jessie,

Well you're lucky tonight
you're first on the list. It does seem
odd to be writing after seeing you last
night, but I just happen to have some
spare time. I'm in an awful humor.
I could eat snakes alive tonight.
The family and I have been chewing
back and forth all day. Dad has
been harping on how much money
I spend and the enormous amount
of gas I use. And Mother has been
nagging about how worthless I am
and so on. I told her tonight that I
am getting sick of loafing around the
poolroom all the time and I won't
come home because it's worse there
with my aunt and her terrible kid.
You know I am extremely hard to
get along with.

Didn't do anything tonight
except hang around. Been listening
to the the radio and still am. H
a Li

Clar
Aug

Dear Jessie,

Well I guess S
going to the races, an
have ordered our tick
said anything to the
may kick. If we do
stop to see you of cou
to date you and your
that night, however
again this week and
for sure.

We at home to

BELL PHONE 77 · R · 3   POST OFFICE BOX 205

CRAMER & BARTOW
"THE CLARION FLYERS"
FLYING FIELD AND HANGARS
CLARION, PA.
ON THE NEW YORK - SAN FRANCISCO AIR MAIL ROUTE

EXHIBITIONS
ADVERTISING
INSTRUCTION

PHOTOGRAPHY
TRANSPORTATION
SALES and SERVICE

Wednesday Evening.

Dear Jessie,

Well things look as if we would
be over Friday night. If anything turns
up to hinder us, I'll call you Friday
morning early. Bill Fowler is coming
along. He says he wants you to date
up Mary Alice Thompson for him. He
also says that he bets she thinks he
is an awful animal (I don't know why)
He likes her a lot.

Bill Cramer has a date in Erie
for that night that he is going to keep.

As ever,
John.

Sinnemahoning, Pa.
Sept. 16, 1925.

Dear Jessie:—

How are you anyway, and where are
you teaching this year? I certainly was
sorry that I could _____ during my
stay in Curwens____
more especially ____
my birthday gree___

I didn't send ___
for I imagined ___
Normal, but I w___
birthday anyway

The reason for ___
If you have ___
book on chemis___
you ___ were t___
can find it, m___

Now listen Jeb___
if you want ___
hesitate to keep ___
why it would ___
me.

My address is just as above — Ginite

Terry.

Lydic House.
Mahaffey, Pa.
March 18, 1925.

Dear Jebbie:—

I know that when you
finish reading this, you're going
to consider me an awful
Lumbbell. Why? Well because
theres only one kint of Pletter
that I know how to write
you, and I cant write that
kind now.

I sure was tickled with
your letter, and to say that
I was glad to talk to you
would be putting it miltly.
I only wish I could see you
and talk to you, alone.

I expect to spend Sunday
in Coalport, so that I can go
to church, and I had hoped

During that first winter while Jessie was designing simple hearts and messages for her students to make valentines, Clarion's John Ditz, one of her constant stream of suitors, had trudged through heavy snow following a storm to purchase a box of candy and a card to present to "Jebbie" on Valentine's Day. Both he and and both were hoping the Jessie were looking forward to an evening together weather would be more favorable near the end of the week. While Jessie was not in love with John, she couldn't help but anticipate their time together as much preferable to cutting out red hearts and white rabbits while sitting in the company of the inquisitive wife of a school director.

A Valentine To My Sweetheart

Someone cares for only you
Cares about the things you do
Someone hopes your heart's glad too
Someone really cares for you.

*I love you
John*

Fortunately the weather broke and on Friday Jessie had her canvas suitcase by the door of the school, barely able to wait until her ride would meet her at the end of the school lane. She had never been so eager to get home because she believed she could not spend another hour in Irishtown or the Fairview school.

As arranged, John arrived Friday evening at seven, candy and card in hand. The valentine was unusually beautiful in an expensive, understated way. A soft pink in tone, the cover was of heavy card stock, the inner sheet of complementary quality, and the envelope lined in silver embossed foil. A pink ribbon threaded through and held the inside sheet to the cover and the message, spare in language and subtle in expression, was underscored by the handwritten closing.

While we know from the contents of the following letter that Terry McGovern wrote regularly to Jessie, we have only the saved letters to confirm his constancy. Older than Jessie by likely two years, in March of 1925 he was working in nearby Mahaffey for the state highway department when he wrote the following:

Dear Jessie,

I know that when you finish reading this you're going to consider me an awful dumbbell. Why? Well, because there's only one kind of letter that I know how to write and I can't write that kind now. I sure was tickled with your letter and to say that I was glad to talk to you would be putting it mildly. I only wish I could see you and talk to you, alone.

I expect to spend Sunday in Coalport, so that I can go to church and I had hoped that you would find it convenient to visit your relatives there, then we could have the whole day together. If anything should turn up that Mr. Shreffler from Clarion[33] can't come, will you please consider my suggestion?

We did mean a lot to each other, didn't we? And now our friendship means just as much to me. The cards we've exchanged have been a source of unlimited pleasure to me and I always want this friendship to continue. I only hope that in the future we can see each other more than we have in the past. I remember distinctly the last time we saw each other. It was September 8, 1923, just before we moved to Emporium.

I don't know who you meant by "Red," the fellow who invited you to the fraternity dance in Carlisle. What is his last name?

Jessie, I'm glad as the dickens that there is nothing serious between you and Winfield.[34] He's a nice enough fellow and I think he and I are friends, but I don't think he's any fellow for you. Personally I kinda like the Schreffler fellow, though I don't think I ever saw him.

Listen, Jessie, now I'll tell you something and I'll ask you something else. I owe you a lot. I met you soon enough after I started to work for the state highway to keep me from acquiring some of the habits of the fellows who work for the state.

Just between you and me, the fellows who work on the Corps for the State are rotten and all they care about a girl is — well, I don't think I have to explain.

I loved you (and I still don't think it was "Puppy Love") enough to keep myself clean for you. That's what I owe you. Do you understand? And now, Jessie, please for the sake of the love we have for each other, and for my sake, please don't get friendly with fellows who work on Corps. If I ever get a chance to talk to you about it I'll try to make you see my point of view.

Lord, didn't we have some good times together? Do you remember "...Theda Bara.[35]" Zuzer had one, too. "Mary Garden"[36] was his. Do you remember the night of the awful wind storm, when we stood on your front porch and I tried to keep you warm?

Ah! I have memories of those days that are terribly dear to me.

I'll be waiting for your call Friday nite sure. As you remember the 13th was our day.

I'm enclosing something I've saved all these years. Do you remember when you wrote it? Will you return it?

Sincerely,

Terry McGovern

Of course, we will never know what Jessie may have written to Terry two years earlier when they evidently were teen-agers (before the term was coined) who were in love.

By the end of the school term in the spring of 1925 Jessie could hardly wait to return to Clarion's college campus and was relieved when her sister chose not to attend the same college. As a returning "collegian" Jessie was even more confident and she made it known to all that she was a second year student and an experienced teacher. She had packed hurriedly, with little of the elaboration demonstrated in her initial trunk stuffing of the previous year.

Upon her arrival on June 21 she went directly to the girls' dormitory, newly renamed Becht Hall in honor of the State Superintendent of Public Instruction. Luxuriating in her surroundings, she quickly crafted a card to tape on her dormitory room door: Jebbie B. Pifer, 148 Becht Hall. She wanted all to know that she had arrived.

The following week Jessie received a post card from Bill Fowler who wrote from the East View Grove Park Inn (a luxury hotel) in Asheville, North Carolina.

June 27, 1925

Dear Jebbie,

The weather is hot here. I miss our special areas of Shady Cook's Forest. Remember? And won't you please write to an old friend?

Always,

Bill

Bill Fowler recently had been graduated from Clarion High School and had started to work for his father. He was slated to enter the University of Pennsylvania in Philadelphia in September and said that he did not want to lose Jessie to any of the "new men on campus" at Clarion. Jessie fully intended to keep Bill's interest, but not to the point of spoiling dates with any other young men. Nearly twenty, Jessie was in no hurry to settle on only one "fella" (another of her favorite new slang words), especially one at a distance, and Philadelphia was definitely at a distance—unless Bill Fowler invited her for a week-end at Penn.

In late June 1925 Jessie received a post card from Bill, a young man she had met on vacation that summer.

> *June 29, 1925*
>
> *Hello, Jessie,*
>
> *I haven't seen a place that reminded me of Curwensville and don't guess I ever will unless I come back to that place. Sure having a good time here but this is the last day here. I am leaving for Miami today. Jess, if you care to write to an old friend you can write me. General Delivery in Miami, Fla. Hope you are having a good time.*
>
> *A friend, Bill*

The first week of August 1925 Jessie received another card from Bill (postmarked Miami). He admits he isn't sure of the spelling of her name, but that did not prevent him from writing.

> *August 3, 1925*
>
> *This may not be the way to spell your name, but guess you will get it just the same. I am glad I met you! 227 Northwest 4th Street, Miami.*
>
> *Bill*

In August after returning home from the Summer Term, Jessie received a letter from **Albert Heston**, written earlier in Coalport, Pennsylvania but mailed from Augusta, Ohio on August 22 with a return address of Mechanicsville, Iowa. Mr. Heston likely had been visiting relatives in Coalport (recall that Jessie also had relatives in Coalport to whom Terry McGovern had referred in any earlier letter) who had tried to arrange a date for Albert with Jessie:

> *Dear Miss Pifer:*
>
> *First of all I suppose apologies are in order. So, with that over, I can say just what I think. Really, I can't remember of ever being so disappointed as last night when you couldn't go. Generally "blind dates" are — well, you can imagine how I, a perfect stranger, would naturally feel toward them. But here, in Pa. blind dates[37] are always good. Just seems all of my friends here have plenty of wonderful girls on whom they can pass off the western friend. So after seeing you last night in the light of a date and later finding you were unable to go, the evening was ruined.*
>
> *This morning Karl and I talked over the possibilities of a Friday night date. But after getting back here with Mother I was informed we were leaving for Rochester today. So, a date with you this year is passé. However, if next year I do get back in the section do you suppose we can arrange for at least one night? Perhaps I might at least hope so. Again, please pardon such informality and if ever you feel inclined I would love to hear from you.*
>
> *Sincerely, Albert Heston, Jr., Mechanicsville, Iowa*

On the same day, August 20, Mr. Heston was composing his letter, John Ditz (Clarion College sender of the pink valentine) was writing from the Hotel Statler in Cleveland, likely on a vacation trip with his parents, persons of means. (John's father was the owner of a large hardware store and a state and national leader in the professional organizations associated with his trade.)

Dear Jessie,

We arrived here yesterday at noon. It is terribly warm. Saw a ballgame yesterday at Dunn Field and a rather risqué musical comedy called "Little Jesse James." The latter was very good, too.

Things aren't going too well. I'm in a bad humor and Dad and I have been arguing right and left. This is a terrible city to drive in due to the extremely large traffic and poor system of management, and also to the fact that people cross the street just wherever and whenever they feel like it.

Sorry that I couldn't take you home yesterday; however, I will probably get over next week to see you. We are going home Friday. Be good and don't flirt too much with other fellows. Write to me at home, Jessie. Don't forget the John "I" (middle initial)[38] part and just address it to Clarion.

As ever,

John

Jessie apparently responded (an activity she did not always relish) and ten days later John wrote:

Well, I guess Shef[39] and I are going to the races,[40] anyways we have ordered our tickets. I haven't said anything to the family yet. They may kick. If we do go, we will stop to see you of course. Shef says to date you and your sister up for that night; however, I will write again this week and let you know for sure.

We got home from Cleveland O.K. Thanks for writing, glad to get it, of course, only it adds one more to my correspondence list and Lord knows I have enough on it already. I took Shef and Haskell for a ride this afternoon. We went over to Punxsy [Punxsutawney] and then to Dubois. We were to a corn roast and picnic the other night that Mother and some of the other ladies had. Another one scheduled tomorrow.

The Clarion County Fair starts Tuesday. Not much of this junk here yet, though I did see the fat lady. She's a whale! Kindly write soon.

As ever yours, John

Jessie received this letter late in the day, as she had been attending a Teachers' Institute in Clearfield all day into evening. At this point she was beginning to look upon John as a good friend rather than a romantic interest, and welcomed his suggestion of a double date so that she would be with "Red" Shreffler just for the sake of dating someone different (Dating many different men was the trend of the times). She still heard from Bill Fowler occasionally, but was not dating him with any regularity.

On Labor Day Jessie had a date with John Ditz and the next morning she headed out to her new school in Hepburnia, relieved that she had found a ride from Curwensville to within walking distance of the school and would not have to board with any of the school directors. She looked forward to having more freedom in the evenings by not being cooped up every evening in a school director's home.

Jessie sought opportunities to attend football games at what she now called her Alma Mater, even though Clarion State Normal School, fifty miles west of Curwensville, was still a small college compared to nearby Penn State College, the same distance to the southeast. She sometimes found a group to travel with to the games at Clarion or State College, either by automobile or train. She could hardly wait to show off her new wardrobe, especially the brand new possum coat she was buying on the payment plan. How she loved that coat and herself in it! She hadn't had it a week before she arranged to have her photo taken wearing the coat, her hair bobbed stylishly, and her lips painted in the current, provocative "bee stung" style.

As a letter of September 8, 1925 shows, Jessie continued her friendship with John Ditz. His personal stationery was as fine in quality as the valentine had been—deckled, monogrammed, and of good weight, another indicator of his social class. John wrote:

Well, you're lucky tonight you're first on the list. It does seem odd to be writing after seeing you last night, but I just happen to have some spare time. I'm in an awful humor. I could eat snakes alive tonight. The family and I have been chewing back and forth all day. Dad has been harping on how much money I spend and the enormous amount of gas I use. And Mother has been nagging about how worthless I am and so on." I told her tonight that I am getting sick of loafing around the poolroom all the time and I won't come home because it's worse there with my aunt and her terrible kid. You know I am extremely hard to get along with.*

I didn't do anything tonight except hang around. Been listening to the radio and still am—a fine orchestra at the Mayflower Hotel in Washington. Just finished reading a couple stories in the "Saturday Evening Post."

What did you mean when you said you had to pack your clothes? Aren't you staying at home? I'd like a date for some night soon with you. I think the coming Sunday night would suit me fine. Let me know and where you are. Would any other night suit you better?

When we got home this morning I found a letter for me and was rather peeved to find that I would now have to go to Kane. Bill [Fowler] has another job now. He is working for the gas company helping to lay the new lines. I have lots I'd like to tell you but can't seem to remember it all. It is one o'clock now and I still have lots to do yet.

As ever John

As classes did not start until the last week of September, it is not unusual that Bill Fowler would still be working until time to leave for Philadelphia. The surprise here is that John rather than Bill is providing this information to Jessie. Jessie, however, still saw Bill occasionally, but not as a serious suitor—but then Jessie rarely considered any one young man as her favorite.

A week later Jessie also heard from Terry McGovern in Sinnemahoning in Cameron County.

September 17, 1925

Dear Jessie,

How are you, anyway, and where are you teaching this year?

I certainly was sorry that I couldn't see you during my stay in Curwensville a few months ago, more especially since I wanted to extend my birthday greetings in person. I didn't send you a card on July 9th for I imagined you were in Lock Haven Normal, but I was thinking of you and wishing you a happy birthday anyway.

The reason for this letter, Jebbie, is that if you have no further use for the chemistry handbook I gave you when you were taking chemistry, and if you can find it, may I have it? Now, listen, Jebbie, if you use it at all, or if you want it for any reason, don't hesitate to keep it, but if you don't need it, it would come in mighty handy to me.

With love, Terry

Terry, at least two years older than Jessie, was enrolled in and working his way through college, toward a degree in mechanical engineering. Likely he was attending Penn State College, considering where he lived and the specialty of the degree (and the possibility that this was an associate's degree). Penn State had had a department of mechanical engineering since 1886 and soon after became one of the ten largest engineering schools in the nation. However, of Terry's many letters to Jessie, most are written from a job location and not a college.

John Ditz also sent Jessie a letter on September 17, this time on letterhead stationery from Cramer & Bartow, "The Clarion Flyers," on the New York, San Francisco Air Mail Route. The Parker Cramer Airfield had been established in 1922 and was the first municipally owned airfield in the U.S., serving as a local strip and as a USPO Airmail emergency field. Cramer himself was the fourth licensed pilot in the entire United States. "Red" Bartow was a local airplane stuntman, in 1924 causing quite a stir by flying under a 322 highway bridge in a bi-plane.

John's letter itself is confirmation that Bill, too, was still playing the field and not dating Jessie exclusively. While Bill likely had met Mary Alice Thompson, a high school classmate of Jessie's, through Jessie, he came to know her better because she was also living in Philadelphia, attending Drexel, a institution that had accepted women since its inception in 1892.

Unlike Drexel, it was not until the establishment of the School of Education in 1914 that the University of Pennsylvania conferred its bachelor's degree on women, and it would be two more decades before the creation of its College of Liberal Arts for Women in 1933 permitted women to take the traditional liberal arts curriculum. For many years women were enrolled in what was named Penn's College for Women before becoming part of the co-ed institution of Penn.[42]

> " . . . in many respects the institution is not equipped to care for you as you should be cared for . . . it is the intention of the University, as soon as money is forthcoming, to develop a College for Women equal to and parallel to the College for Men."
>
> *The Record Book 1925,* Yearbook for the College of Women. p.5.

September 17, 1925

Dear Jessie,

Well, things look as if we would be over Friday night. If anything turns up to hinder us, I'll call you Friday morning early. Bill Fowler is coming along. He says he wants you to date up Mary Alice Thompson for him. He also says that he bets she thinks he is an awful animal. He likes her a lot, which suits me fine.

As ever, John

The fall term could not go fast enough for Jessie. She could barely contain her excitement at the invitation she had recently received to spend the entire Thanksgiving vacation in Philadelphia with a college friend whose brother attended the University of Pennsylvania and, as luck would have it where Jessie was involved, the brother had met Jessie in early August. Like almost every other young man who ever met her, George L. Thomas liked what he saw. He had convinced his sister that she and her friend Jessie should come visit him at Penn over the Thanksgiving vacation. Thus, an invitation was extended to both young women; reservations for the women would be made at a reputable hotel, and the college men from Penn pledged utmost respect.

Jessie pleaded with her mother, "The Thanksgiving football game is just about the biggest thing ever, Mary Jane and I will room together, and ride down on the train, and probably also visit Mary Alice Thompson, and see the Liberty Bell and maybe a real Broadway play, and go to John Wanamaker's store, and I promise we will find a church to attend on Sunday."

The day before Thanksgiving, school closed at 11:30 a.m. and by 3:00 p.m. Jessie was at the train station at the end of Curwensville where she boarded for Clearfield. There she met Mary Jane, coming in from Clarion by way of Dubois to Clearfield. The two friends traveled to Tyrone where they purchased their tickets for Philadelphia at $1.65 a seat. They arrived at the Broad Street Station where they were met by George Thomas and his roommate Henry Allen, both with bright smiles.

Even though it was midnight, the two couples stopped at Horn and Hardart for a late night supper. Always parlaying, Jessie calmly said to George, "You go first," never admitting she had no idea how to place the coin, open the little door, and retrieve a food selection.

On Thanksgiving morning the fellows met the girls in the hotel lobby and the four of them headed for Franklin Field where Jessie could pretend for the moment that she was a full-time, true co-ed. As the four friends entered the stadium on South Thirty-third Street, Jessie's attention was drawn to the sound of a brass band and freshmen in their beanies who were distributing copies of the original "Freshman Song." Best of all, Penn defeated Cornell, 7 – 0, leaving the two young couples in an even merrier frame of mind.

The rest of the week-end was filled with sightseeing in Center City—including the active billboards of Sherwin-Williams and Morning Sip Coffee, seeing Willie Howard in *Sky High* at the Chestnut Street Opera House and *The Harem* at the Broad Street Theatre, listening to a pipe organ concert at John Wanamaker's, and dining and dancing to the music of Billy Hayes at the popular Cathay Tea Garden.

As promised, on Sunday morning the couples attended the 10:30 a.m. worship service at Asbury University Church on the campus of Penn, made a final stop at Horn and Hardart for breakfast, picked up their luggage, and headed for the railroad station where Jessie and Mary Jane kissed their dates, and boarded their Pullman car for the return trip to Tyrone where they would change trains and head for home. However, before they arrived at the Tyrone station, Jessie made the acquaintance of Edmund Smith whose address has been immortalized on a slip of paper pasted in the *Girl Graduate*, along with the ticket stubs, playbills, book of amusements, and her hand-written notation in the corner of the display ad for the Cathay Tea Room: "Hot place."

George's letter in response to Jessie's thank you note said it all,

December 3, 1925

Dear Jessie,

Never in a million years did I imagine the euphoric week-end we shared. You are one amazing gal and I think I am in love with you. No, let me reword that. I AM in love with you! When may I see you again?"

With Love and Admiration,

George

Likely Jesse did not continue a correspondence with George, as no other letters are in evidence.

The following July Jessie returned to Clarion for her third summer, continuing to accumulate credits for permanent teacher certification. While she was there, the ever-devoted Terry McGovern sent her a birthday card on July 6, 1926 from Angola, Indiana to Jessie's rooming house at 1075 E. Main Street, so that it would arrive by July 9, Jessie's twenty-first birthday.

With two years of teaching experience behind her, Jessie was even more self-confident and independent, viewing the summer classes as something necessary and the summer social life as very appealing and liberating. Jessie and a classmate from the previous year rented a double room in a private home rather than living in the dormitory.

Jessie continued to carry her *Girl Graduate* memory book with her, and on August 18, 1926 the following messages, typical of the time, were inscribed on its pages:

"You couldn't forget a devil like me." –John White, Echo, Penna.

"...don't forget the good old times we had in rooms 56 and 59 Becht Hall during summer of '26. Oh, those Hot Dates???"   – Melva Leach, 1051 So. Brady St., DuBois

"On a hill there is a rock. Printed on this is "forget-me-not." – Dave Kinter

"Dearest Jessie, To attempt to tell you how much I enjoyed your delightful companionship during this summer term would be useless indeed."   —Bill Cramer [43]

"Don't forget our hot dates together, Friday, August 20. – Gene Conrad.

Just a token of friendship to the nicest and sweetest lady in the world. Clark M. Bunnell

And, of course, flowers arrived regularly from various admirers.

At Clarion Normal School Jessie and **Joe Goodwin**, along with an ever-widening circle of friends and acquaintances, always were devising activities by which they could have good times without necessarily being "paired off." Occasionally a group of these friends would head for Cook's Forest near Clarion. The old Cook Forest Inn might be their destination, a bit rundown, but available for a meal. From there they could walk to the fire tower from which they could have a panoramic view of the forest. If they felt particularly adventuresome and had dressed for hiking, they could find a bluff from which to view the Clarion River, so named for the sound of the ripple made by the river.

The collegians might also stop near the old natural mineral springs, once known as Seneca Trail Mineral Springs where visitors bathed and drank the spring waters believed to have curative powers. However, in most cases the only curative liquid the Clarion Normal School students were interested in is what could be found in their hip flasks.

Five weeks before Labor Day was the traditional time for the annual Clearfield County Fair and Jessie never missed this event, particularly the harness races to which her father had introduced her many years before. Jessie had no trouble finding escorts and on the rare afternoons when no one was available, she took herself to the races, striking up a conversation with whoever happened to be sitting nearby, especially if the whoever happened to have binoculars.

Jessie continued to live at home, as girls and women of any age didn't leave home unless they got married. To flounce off to a boarding house or an apartment would have been unheard of. While that attitude would soon change throughout America, in the early and mid-twenties in small towns a female adult lived with her parents or other relatives until she married.

By the end of the decade, however, more single women in cities began to move out of their homesteads into small kitchenette apartments, but in smaller towns one was lucky to find anything other than a three-five room apartment or a rooming house. Jessie could not have afforded an apartment and renting a room held little appeal. She asked, "Why would I want to rent a room in someone's house? It would be worse than boarding with the school directors when I first started teaching." She was too busy, she said, to take care of an apartment. Besides, at her age, everyone expected she soon would be married. Heaven knew she had more than enough suitors.

On Saturdays in small towns stores were open through the evening hours. On the rare Saturday evening that Jessie didn't have a date or other plans with friends, she liked to sashay down the street and after browsing through the main area, visit the shoe department of Kovac's Department Store where she would invariably ask for some new shoe fashion that had not yet reached the small towns. "Bill," as she might say to the owner's son, "aren't you going to get in any of those smart walking shoes?" Bill would blush, hoping his father wasn't noticing his obvious crush on Jessie, and say, "Miss Pifer, I will order anything you want."

Jessie's typical response was, "Well, let me think about it. I may try the stores in Altoona the next time I am there." She would then flounce out the side entrance and walk to the corner to cross State Street to the Park Hotel, then at the Fire Hall turn left on North Street. By that route she could see into the back yard of the Howard J. Thompson residence on the chance that Mary Alice would be around.

Jessie sometimes felt a bit envious of "Tommy," having a wonderful life as a full-time coed at Drexel, with striking, custom-made clothes —even a real raccoon coat. Jessie tried to tell herself that it was not the coat, nor the shoes, nor the beautifully beaded evening purse that bothered her—even though the coat was just what Jessie would have bought for herself had she been able to afford it. Mary Alice's coat had come from the fine Bonwit Teller Department Store in Philadelphia. "It's a wonder she didn't go to Mawsan & DeMany," Jessie sulked, recalling the fine fur store she had seen a year ago. She began to think of a way she could get Tommy to invite her to Drexel for a week-end. She certainly knew how to get there by train. "I'll work on that," she told herself, holding her head high as she turned down Thompson Street headed for home.

Most of the time Jessie wasn't the least bit interested in becoming *serious* about *anyone*. Joe Goodwin, among others, still pursued her, but he found a long distance relationship difficult to maintain. On October 27, 1926 Joe wrote,

Dear Jebbie,

For the love of Mike, how can anyone get you on the phone? I have tried, by actual count, seven hundred and forty-six times. Tried twice tonight. The operator told me that the number was a printing shop and they were closed after six o'clock and so could not call anyone to the phone. I was in Dubois Sunday but again couldn't get you on the phone and as I didn't have a car couldn't come to Curwensville.

May I come over to see you over the week-end? If I may come, I will be there at about seven-thirty or eight o'clock Saturday evening. Will you call me up Friday at six o'clock and tell me whether I can come or not. Our phone number is 398.

Please let me come.

Love,

Joe Goodwin

While there is no record assuring that Jessie returned Joe's call, his interest in her remained, as this letter indicates. The return address holds only his initials, JWG, Jr. and a company name, BBG Co.[44] Clarion, PA:

Dear Jebbie,

Well, the company sent me to Detroit this morning. I was supposed to come to Curwensville. They told me at nine and I had to leave at ten so I had them send the telegram from the office.[45] I have been traveling around ever since. I am sorry I couldn't come over that Saturday but it was impossible. I am also sorry I couldn't let you know sooner but I didn't know myself. Am I forgiven?

Did you enjoy the football game at State? I was in Chicago last Saturday and was lucky enough to see Army and Navy play. I would rather see the cadets and midshipmen <u>parade</u> than watch them play football.

May I come to Curwensville to see you this Saturday? If you will let me I will come - job or no job. Please let me come. Will you be in the telephone office Wednesday night at seven-thirty so I can call you up? Please write to me.

Love, Joe

Jessie was far too busy to worry about writing to someone in Detroit or wondering if he would be able to reach her by telephone. There were dresses to hem and stockings to buy, for by the middle of the decade the amount of fabric in a woman's outfit had decreased by half and had gone from amply cut ankle-length dresses over such underpinnings as corset covers, envelope chemises, and petticoats to dress styles designed to make the wearer look as pencil-slim as possible, knee-length over silk or artificial silk (later known as "rayon") undergarments.

Stockings and lingerie made from rayon gained great popularity because the fabric more easily conformed to the shape of the body—particularly hips and legs—than did cotton. Young women in particular had gone from daytime stockings of cotton or lisle to silk or rayon stockings of a flesh color. Less fragile and not as expensive as silk, rayon flesh-colored stockings soon became as standard as the short skirt that allowed them to be noticed.

By 1927 mah-jongg had become a world craze, and there were 25 million radios in use in the United States. Forty percent of homes in the United States had telephones, every third home had a radio, and two-thirds had electricity.[46] The typical employed factory worker had a third more real purchasing power than in 1914 and the installment plan allowed the worker, who might not have saved his money for a purchase, to buy what he wanted. Soon after, most merchants offered an "easy payment plan."

New Hotel Logan
(OPPOSITE POST OFFICE)
GEO. H. SLOPPY, PROPRIETOR
DUBOIS, PA.

Thursday Eve.

My dear Jessie:—

I did not forget my promise that I made concerning the letter that I was suppose to write last evening, but just when I was ready to write to you I was called on the phone to sell a young fellow a new suit and some furnishings. This kept me until after eleven o'cl... ...d I did not get it ... trust that you ... me, honey. I stay... town for dinner ... and since it is ... night out, thoug... would be better ... while here and ... trip down later ...

RONALD CORBETT
PRESIDENT
J. L. FITZ GERALD
SEC'Y & TREAS.

A.G. CORBETT DRUG CO.
DRUGS, BOOKS AND STATIONERY
Home address, 79 Wansee St.
Crafton, Pa.   CLARION, PA. 9/20/27

Dear Jessie,

This sure is terrible paper to use after you write to me on such fine stationery but I can't afford any better.

How is school by now? Formal is terrible this term. No good looking girls like you to take your place and everything is so dead around here without you that I just can't stand it any longer so I am leaving here this Saturday.

I am going back to Dormont and work where I had been a year ...

B. R. CUMMINGS CO.
"Quality Clothes"
25 W. Long Ave., Dubois, Pa.

Friday Eve.

My dear Tessie:—

I am not laughing and believe me have never done so about anything that concerns you dear. When I came in this evening I found your letter awaiting me and the accusation that you think me somewhat of a civilian. One that might be found in a play; a fellow that tries to win a girl, and during this period sh...

1927
...iepois, Pa.

...is just 10.30.
...ished all my
...evening; so I'm
...do just break
...mise to you,
...this letter in
...this evening. Arrived
Sunday evening at
thirty, as it was a
night to drive, and
only regret was that
...here not along.
About my coming over this
...eek I am still at a
...loss to know just what

Aug 9, 1927
Broadway, Pa.

Dear Jessie

Just a note to let you and Al know that I tried to call Tom last night and couldent get him on the phone so I think that if Al craves him She had better try and get him herself. And say old thing I came in from work last night expecting a nice long letter there from the only one and didnt find it. Well dear I had to get up 15 minutes early to wright this and see I will have to make it short as the gang has just arrived.

Yours and everything Don.

P.s. will wright more tonight

Because telephone communication was not always reliable (not all private homes had telephones and one either had to rely on neighbors for messages or use the public phone at the telephone company office), telegrams or special delivery letters were often used if a message needed to reach a person faster than a regular letter would be sent and delivered. An example is **Dan Campbell** from Brockway, who had been a classmate of Jessie's at Clarion. Dan sent her this letter to the home where Jessie was boarding c/o William Kissel, Liberty Street, using Special Delivery (10¢). Like many of her suitors he mentions he is hoping to hear from her.

> August 9, 1927
> Brockway, PA
>
> Dear Jebbie,
>
> I tried to call Tom last night and couldn't get him on the phone so I think that if Alice craves him she should try and get him herself. And say, old thing, I came in from work last night expecting a nice long letter here from the only one who matters (you, of course), and didn't find it. Well, dear, I had to get up 15 minutes early to write this and see I will have to make it short as the gang has just arrived.
>
> > Yours and everything, Dan
>
> P.S. Will write more tonight

The next gentleman caller to appear on the scene was **Neal Buchanan** whose home was DuBois where he worked as a haberdasher and apparently lived with his parents. The relationship between Jessie and Neal Buchanan is here in its early stages, as Neal indicates.

> My dearest Jessie: --
>
> It is just 10:30—and I have finished all my work for the evening; so in order that I do not break another promise to you, must get this letter in the mail this evening. Arrived home Sunday evening at twelve-thirty, as it was a dandy night to drive, and my only regret was that you were not along.

About my coming over this week I am still at a loss to know just what night to say that I can come over. As I tried to explain last Sunday evening, all my time must be devoted to our interests in Du Bois for at least three more weeks. After that I can plan ahead what nights are suitable to you for seeing me. I know, dear little girl, that you understand my interest at the present in doing all that is within my power to help.

If you have not made plans for next Sunday I sure would like to come over, but should this not be the case, please let me know and I will try my best to have a night off later in the week. It doesn't seem right that we should not see each other for an entire week, and I do not wish it to be, dear.

Please write to me soon as I shall expect to hear from you.

Love, Neal Buchanan

A week later Neal's letter indicates that Jessie and he are seeing each other and a romance appears to have blossomed. It also implies that Neal was campaigning for a candidate in a primary election, a contentious one that fall.

My dear Jessie,

As I am writing this letter you are no doubt enjoying the dance at the park this evening. Gee! I wish that I were there, too. The night is perfect and what a glorious moon to help one enjoy the pleasures of living. Of course, I realized that there are times when a fellow cannot have everything he wishes for; therefore, I should feel happy in the fact that we were together last evening. It seems that the more a person gets in this day and age, the more each of us expects.

Then, too, dear girlie, I must not forget how good you have been to me; in allowing the last two Sunday evenings to be mine. Boy, oh boy! but I have looked forward to them, and although at times I have failed to please you, as I readily know when this happens, still my only desire is to be uppermost in your thoughts. Some day I may be lucky enough to attain this desire, but not at the present. That I feel sure.

When I left Sunday evening you said that I could call to see you this coming Wednesday. I trust that this arrangement is still satisfactory for, Jessie, I am looking forward to seeing you again this week. As soon as the primary election is over

I want you to visit us during some weekend.

Tomorrow your school begins and no doubt you will be quite busy getting settled. Write to me real soon, dear, and tell me how the first day rated in school. Also anything about yourself as it is very much _you_ that interests me.

Love, Neal

Around the same time Jessie also heard from **Bob Schauwecker** who lived in Dormont (near Pittsburgh) and was attending Clarion Normal School where he boarded in a rooming house run by a Mrs. Murphy. He, like many other young men attending Clarion, was working at the popular A.G. Corbett Drugstore. His newsy letter likely was welcomed, but his next letter does not appear until the following spring.

September 20, 1927

Dear Jebbie,

This sure is terrible paper to use after you write to me on such fine stationery, but I can't afford any better.

How is school by now? Normal is terrible this term. No good looking girls like you to take your place and everything is so dead around here without you that I just cant stand it any longer so I am leaving here this Saturday.

I am going back to Dormont [near Crofton] and work where I had been a year ago.

Bo[47] just told me to tell you that he still loves you. Now I'm really jealous and won't stand for this much longer. There is altogether too much competition, "Bo" - Don Port & J. By the way, Don was in here a few days ago and I met him. He said that he had heard about me from some female so I have been wondering since what you might have told him. He sure is a big brute.

How is Camp Anchor Inn? You failed to mention in your letter whether you had a good time there the next evening, but it sure isn't your fault if the person with you does not have a good time, Jebbie. You are such a good sport. I just couldn't help thinking a lot of you.

I wish you were over here at your aunt's in DuBois[48] as I would like very much to see you before I go. "Bo" and I thought we might find a way whereby we could come over to see you this week-end and also bring "Al" over, but as yet we do not know. If anything turns up we will call you on the phone.

45

You will hardly know the store when next you see it as the ceiling has been newly painted and they will finish putting on the wallpaper today.

Well, Jebbie, are you coming here to Normal next year? In case we don't get over this week it may be that I won't see you until next summer when you come here to school.

As you know, Dan Campbell has gone to State. He is coming down to my home for Thanksgiving.

Well, Jebbie, I must close as it is 1:30 p.m. and Jim is due back.

Take care of yourself and drop me a line soon.

Always, Bob

P.S. I just heard that Betty Wray is in a family way. What do you know about it?

The next time we hear from Neal is three weeks after his previous letter of September 5. It appears that there had been a misunderstanding, one he handled with grace. Further is evidence that Bill Fowler may now have been in a serious relationship with Jessie, at least in the opinion of Neal.

September 24, 1927

My dear Jessie: --

I am not laughing and believe me have never done so about anything that concerns you, dear. When I came in this evening I found your letter awaiting me and the accusation that you think me somewhat of a villain. One that might be found in a play; a fellow that tries to win a girl, and, during this period, shows her a glimpse of his true self such as you seemed to gather from last Wednesday evening's date with me.

This was far, far from my intentions; for the longer anybody knows me I feel sure they will say I try my best to play fair in every respect. When I said that this would be our last date I was not thinking of myself but of you. Once before you told me that you and Bill [Fowler] were more than friends to each other, and again on Wed. evening when you said that he had written you concerning myself, and felt sure that he could trust you; why it seemed to me as if I had over stepped. Therefore, the better way for me to avoid any trouble between you two appeared best for me to get out.

You see, Jessie, while he is away at school trying hard to obtain his desired goal, he certainly must wish you to be a pal and a help to him until he has finished. If the merits possessed in me are not enough to have you like me with Bill at home and with the same chance of seeing you as I have; then I must be a friend and nothing more.

I have worked hard, Jessie, the last few weeks, and my visits to see you were becoming more and more a desire than a pleasure. A desire, for I could forget everything of the day's happenings and just be with you. It seemed as if two defeats within forty-eight hours was more than I had bargained for.

I trust that you may understand this better, Jessie, and that we may be good pals to each other. Every thought of mine was been spoken to you in truth.

Love, Neal

Neal's next letter of indicates a growing devotion and love. It also reveals the bad winters in Clearfield County and the difficulties travel entailed at a time before the maintenance of rural roads was taken over by the Commonwealth in 1931.

December 6, 1927

My dearest Jessie,

About four-thirty Mother called me on the phone to tell me that a letter had arrived from you. You see, even she seemed to know that I was put out by not being able to see you last Sunday. They left everything up to me; whether I should make the trip or not, and knowing that both Dad and Mother would worry while I was gone, I called at four o'clock to tell you that I would not be there. When I did not get you I asked Mother to let you know that I would call at seven that evening.

Now, darling, if there had not been so many wrecks near us, very likely I would have made the trip. I like both my Mother and Dad a whole lot, dear, and I love you with all my heart, but honestly the condition of the roads scared me out. If it had been a case of absolute necessity I would have been there with you if I had to walk.

However, I will be over Tuesday evening at eight o'clock without fail for I want to see you so much, and each day that I am away makes life just that much longer.

Soon after this letter reaches you I will be there to tell you what I seem unable to write here. Please forgive me for not writing more, but I have to go back to work for a few hours and also to break a stag engagement that I made the other day.

With the most of love, Neal

Three days later Neal writes to explain why he had not written the previous evening as he had promised. He asks to see Jessie the coming Saturday. His even tone is evident.

December 9, 1927

My dearest Jessie,

I did not forget my promise that I made concerning the letter that I was supposed to write last evening, but just when I was ready to write to you I was called on the phone to sell a young fellow a new suit and some furnishings. This kept me until after eleven o'clock and I did not get it done. I trust that you will forgive me, honey, I stayed down town for dinner this evening and since it is such a terrible night out, thought that it would be better to write while here and save an extra trip down later on.

No doubt you saw in the morning paper that Alice and Chuck were married yesterday in Punxey. It was quite a surprise to me as I did not expect that it was as serious as all that. However, I wish them all the joy of a happy married life. By the way, this evening about four-thirty I saw Alice on the street, but did not get an opportunity to congratulate her.

Oh, yes, the Sandy [Township] High School was badly damaged by fire about three-thirty this afternoon, and I suppose the pupils are all happy that they do not have to go to school. Outside of these few items there is nothing new in the "burg."

I would like to come over this Sunday evening and if it should not meet with your schedule, drop me a card Friday night; otherwise I will be on hand at about eight o'clock.

Am working hard and must go home now, as I have not been there since morning and you know "Mother's Boy" should not stay out so late in the evening.

With Lots of Love,

Neal

Three weeks later we view a comfortable relationship of a young man longing to see his girl. Neal tells Jessie how much he wants to be with her.

December 28, 1927

My dear Jessie,

I told you when I came over Monday eve that it was a bad habit in the making for me to have so many dates together; however, Tuesday night I went to the show. I wondered that evening just what my girlie was doing and Oh! boy, the temptation was strong to be with you once again.

Today our boss decided that we are about ready to take inventory and you know what that means: plenty of good hard work for all of us the next few days. Well, the sooner we get started the sooner it is over.

It looks like I will have to go to Pittsburgh next Monday morning, but I am not going to miss next Sunday night's date with you for anything. I too look forward to these nights with eagerness as they mean so much to me.

Everything is going along smoothly as business is far duller than before Christmas. A good many of the boys who are away at school drop in to see us, including Bill Moorhead and his wife. Bill is getting along fine in New York and I hope he makes good for he is one fine boy in my estimation.

The dances are being quite well attended, in fact too well for a chance to do any dancing.

Drop me a line this week, Jessie, and write about anything in particular. You can make it a short or a long letter just as you wish for it helps to make the time pass more quickly for me when I hear from you.

I will be over Sunday evening to help you celebrate the first of the New Year.

Love,

Neal

49

If I could find a garden
Where all the
Sweethearts grew
I'd look 'em over...every one,
And then I'd just pick YOU.

B. R. CUMMINGS CO.

"Quality Clothes"

25 W. LONG AVE., DUBOIS, PA.

Feb. 6, 1928.

My dearest Jessie:-

Well here goes for the long delayed letter, which I trust you will still appreciate; even tho I am a terrible correspondent and a dull one at that. Practise makes perfect they .... I do more writing to yo......... more proficien...... help me to ...... your opinio......

Just a ...... night. Di...... thing to y...... that make...... You know ...... always be...... like that ......

JD

Dear Jessie,

You said once that you would always be a friend. Friends, of course, take an interest in each others health and pleasures. How are you and what is all the news? Would you write?

John.

Punxsutawney, Pa.
May 20-27.

Dear Gibbie,
I'll bet you will be
surprised to hear from me,
but really I've intended
to write for some time, but
just kept putting it off—you
know me. How are
you anyway? Have you
been doing anything out
of the ordinary this last
winter? I am still
going with Andy and
everything is quite the
same as before. I saw
Al & Chuck today. Had
Andy out for a ride.
You know I can drive
now and that helps
a little.
Listen old dear, are
you going to school
this summer? If so
where? I haven't decided
just yet what I will
do, but am going somewhere.

Sat. Noon.

, It seemed so nice
you once again.
te intervening
years. Some
ith your first
tty stationery.
w style of
? It isn't so
e you used to use.
be this will be
a diary, who
t of all it is
d is for your
t to write—
so many things
have happened since we saw
each other last, but are they of

Letters Letters Letters Letters
1928 1928 1928 1928 1928 1928 1928 1928 1928 1928 1928 1928 1928

The new year of 1928 brought with it John Ditz's fervent pursuit of Jessie, followed by Terry McGovern's strong devotion and Neal's ardor. At times it was the actual physical distance that made things difficult for these three young men (but less so for Jessie, because the odds were in her favor that on any given week-end at least one of them would be available), but mostly it was the emotional distance Jessie often established by not responding to the letters she received that made it difficult for the men to confirm their plans with her.

John Ditz frequently became impatient with Jessie's not replying to his letters. On February 6, 1928 he wrote from McKean Dorm at the University of Pennsylvania, where he was in his junior year.

> *February 6, 1928*
>
> *Dear Jessie,*
>
> *You said once that you would always be a friend. Friends, of course, take an interest in each other's health and pleasures. How are you and what is all the news? Would you write?*
>
> *John*

One reason Jessie might have been ignoring John's pleas was that she was spending more time with Neal. She received his letter the same day as John's arrived.

> *February 6, 1928*
>
> *My dearest Jessie,*
>
> *Well, here goes for the long-delayed letter, which I trust you will still appreciate; even though I am a terrible correspondent and a dull one at that. Practice makes perfect they say, and, if I do more writing, perhaps I may become more proficient. Then again it may help me to a better advantage in your opinion of me. Hey what?*
>
> *Just a word—about the other night. Did your Mother say anything to you about*

the light? That makes my heart act so queer. You know honey bunch I have always been afraid of something like that happening, and I want so much to be just the right sort of a companion that your parents would trust you with. Gee! I hope that we did not make a mistake; for I like you as I have so often said to you and for some reason or other I cannot quit thinking about last evening. I know what you will say, "forget it," but sometimes that is hard to do, dear.

So the next three evenings you are going to spend at the Chautauqua[49] and I shall visit the club until Thursday evening and then back to the "burg" to see you again. Oh Boy! it sure is nice to have a girl like you who looked so nice as you did last night, and that's no apple sauce.

Think of me once in awhile, dearest, and I will surely be over on Thursday.

                                        With loads of love, Neal

Ten days later, Neal writes again, with an apology that he had not written sooner. He must, however, have felt confident enough in their relationship to explain he couldn't see her this particular evening as planned but wants to see her later in the week.

February 15, 1928

My dearest Jessie,

I am sorry that I did not write sooner this week as I promised, but we have been so busy at the store. Tomorrow is dollar day in Du Bois and as you very likely know it means plenty of work for yours truly.

I will not be able to see you this evening as today is the 15th of the month and we keep open till after 8 o'clock in the evening. I did not think of this when I talked to you on the phone last Sunday or I would not have made this arrangement. However, if it is at all possible I would like to come over this Friday, but if it should interfere with your plans just drop me a card.

It is my lunch time, so cannot say all that I would like to, dear, so just remember that I send

                                        My best Love, Neal

Perhaps Neal might have been more expressive of his love had he known that the day before Jessie had received an obviously expensive Valentine from John Ditz, followed by a long letter sent three days later. We can assume that Jessie wrote to John after receiving the card (this in the days when letters were picked up at drop boxes several times a day and delivered twice a day).

February 18, 1928

My dear Jessie,

It seemed so nice to hear from you once again. As you say, the intervening time was like years. Some class to you with your fur coat and pretty stationery. But why the new style of handwriting? It isn't so nice as the one you used to use.

Maybe this will be a book, perhaps a diary, who knows? But most of all it is a letter to you and is for your enjoyment. What to write—that's hard—so many things have happened since we saw each other last, but are they of importance? Some great poet once said that no matter how great a sorrow, or hurt, or anguish one might suffer at some time, it is soon forgotten and unfelt in the flow of life.

Rather than go a long ways back it will be perhaps better to start with Xmas. I almost had my mind made up to come over and look you up, but didn't for several reasons. I didn't know how I would be received for one, and, for another, the week between Xmas and New Year's I drove down to Pittsburgh and Wheeling and out into Ohio on a little trip by myself. When I returned the weather had set in bad again and the family was peeved at my going away and staying so long. Hence travelling east was sort of postponed till Easter.

An outline would be a help in writing this for I'm sure there will be a lot of things I'll forget to tell you. Maybe I had better save something for the next time anyway.

After I wrote you the note the idea of calling up Mary Alice hit me. She didn't have much to say except that you hadn't written to her for a long time. She told me that Marjorie and Alice Wall were down here.

Speaking of old time acquaintances, do you remember Marguerite Sullivan that used to go to the Normal? Had a note from her last week. A fellow from her home town that I know here gave her my address. She says Hilda Nicholson is going to Slippery Rock Normal, too. Did you know her? I can't place her.

It's snowing pretty hard but is melting right off. The weather here is as bad and as changeable as ever.

Dad has been here all week, but I haven't seen much of him. As ever, he and I aren't on very good terms. Same old reason. Yesterday afternoon, I took him out to look over the new Auburns.[50] That's what I'm yelling for now, but try and get it. Last night he took me to a banquet that didn't go half bad. The restaurants around here are as bad as ever.

Our basketball team has been going pretty good. They won seven straight up till Thursday night. A day was due to come when the star shooter would be off form and he sure was rotten that night for he couldn't even hit the backboard. They play Harvard here tonight.

I never miss a game. The Freshman team was a wonder until the two best players on it flunked out.

More fellows flunked out this semester than ever before. Something like 300, so they say. I got four Gs and three Ps which is way above my usually running. Guess I'm getting more conscientious; at any rate I'm working more.

I've seen only seven shows this year (due to a grave shortage of finances):

"Five O'clock Girl" – a good musical comedy

"The Connecticut Yankee" – an even better musical comedy

"Broadway" – a wonderful drama

"The Cardboard Lover" – a good farce with Jeanne Eagels in the lead

"Immoral Isabella" – a parody on Columbus and Isabella, very smutty and funny even though strictly censored here.

"The Barker" – a dandy drama of circus life

"The Spider" – a good mystery play.

Haven't even seen many movies.

This is getting to be too long and I have to run downtown. Please write me a nice, long answer. I miss you.

As ever,
John

February continued to be a bonanza month of letters for Jessie with a note card from Terry McGovern, asking her to write. Had he known the high competition he was facing from other suitors, he likely would have written a longer letter.

February 22, 1928

Dear Jessie: --

Have you answered my letter yet? If you haven't, please do. I'm watching the mails for a letter.

Last nite after writing to you I read all the letters that I still have from you. I have the first one you ever wrote to me and the last six. Do you remember the first one? In case you don't, I am enclosing the envelope. It's pretty sadly worn now. But then, it's almost 6 ½ years old now.

Always,

Terry

The envelope Terry refers to was found enclosed in this letter, postmarked Grampian and Tyrone, RPO[51], 1921. Terry was correct in saying he had kept her letter for 6 ½ years, an indication of the devotion he held for her.

Terry, ever faithful and honest to a fault, wrote again the following day, cautiously giving Jessie an excuse not to write if she doesn't want to continue corresponding with him.

February 23, 1928

Dear Jessie: --

And along came George, so you see I cannot tell a lie. This really is from me, and though I don't deserve an answer, I hope I'll get one.

In spite of all that, Jessie, whatever you do don't ever get the idea that you'd like the South. Frankly, I'll tell you, it's impossible. I know you never would like it.

But to get on with the story, if you don't intend to answer this, won't you please drop me a note and let me know that it's useless for me to expect an answer.

And anyhow, it rained today as you see eggs are 27 cents per dozen.

Again, I must continue. Last December I graduated and now you'd never recognize me. For you see I'm different. Now I'm a Mechanical Engineer. What do you know about that? Anyway it's so.

I'm working for the Missouri Pacific RR. We call it the MOP, taking a special apprentice course and I don't know whether I'll ever finish it or not 'cause I don't like the South at all, and this is why. Down here most all the fellows call girls "gals" and I don't like that, do you?

I've been down here since the 6th of January and in that short time I've had about three weeks' sickness. I just can't seem to get acclimated and I jump from one terrible cold to another. Once I just missed pneumonia by about - that much. (That isn't very much, is it?)

Where are you teaching school now and how do you like it? And say thanks for the Xmas card. I treasure it still.

Do you remember Jettie, the little dis-arguable fight we had over your uke once? And, anyway, please answer this 'cause I dreampt about you the night before last, and when I get your answer another letter will leave here for there from me to you right away.

Always,
Jerry

By the late 1920s the automobile had clearly changed the face of America and the way people traveled. In addition to affecting mass transportation, especially rail travel, the young people of this period were the first to have wider opportunities to meet one another because of automobiles. More importantly it affected the interaction between and among people, where they went and what they did—in and out of the vehicle.

For men and women in their twenties the car became a room on wheels—storm-proof, lockable, and parkable all day and all night in all kinds of weather. The closed car was in effect a room protected from the weather and could be occupied at any time of the day or night and moved at will into a darkened byway or a country lane.[52] From the standpoint of youth, the automobile offered an almost universally available means of escaping temporarily from the supervision of parents and chaperones, as well as neighborhood opinion.

The automobile provided privacy and the means by which the personal relationships became more physical. It is the automobile that led to the proliferation of necking and petting, or as those of the era called it, "parking." It also didn't take long for young men to learn the knack of "one arm driving," the term coined for driving with one arm around the girl sitting close to the driver.[53]

Many of Jessie's suitors were either up and coming young working men whose jobs required an automobile or college students who were from families that could afford to buy cars for their sons, so there was little concern for Jessie about having places to go on a date.

As a working girl, Jessie had opportunities to follow the times – jumping into a car (although not yet one of her own) and driving off at a moment's notice—without asking anyone's permission—to dance in another town twenty miles away, where there were strangers and she could have enjoyed a freedom impossible in her own neighborhood—or, if she agreed, to go "parking."

Even with—or perhaps because of—this freedom, Jessie was torn between her religious upbringing and the religious skepticism that seemed to accompany the new, relaxed social code. She liked to count herself among those young men and women who prided themselves on their modern-mindedness in which there was a disposition to regard church work or social service work or anything else to which the word "uplift" could be applied as an unwarranted intrusion upon other people's privacy. "Besides, one had a right to enjoy oneself," Jessie thought, "and taking a ride in a car on a clear Sunday morning was much more fun than going to church."

Stinging because Papa forbade her to accept dates on Sunday mornings, Jessie was disgruntled that many of the young men she knew could be found on the golf links rather than in their church pews. She likely muttered to herself, "No wonder the church is losing hold of the brighter members of my generation." She no doubt questioned herself—and her father—as to why her friends could plan an all day event on Sunday and she couldn't go on a date until after Sunday dinner, typically served in her home between 1:00 and 1:30 p.m. This was particularly hindering in dating a young man from a nearby town on a Sunday, as noted in John Ditz's question as to when he can see her on Easter Sunday…..

February 27, 1928

My dear Jessie,

Mark me down for Easter.[54] I'll be over for sure. I had intended to come whether invited or not. You know a bad penny always turns up again so I'll be there with bells on. I'm anxious to see you. How soon do you think you can get away? "

I had wanted to answer your letter as soon as it came but in the rush of events it had to be postponed. Last night Ed took me over to Drexel to a dance. It was a blind date and pretty sad. Saw Mary Alice. Only talked to her a short while. Told her you would write. Was that O.K.? By the way, how is your sister getting along with Tommy's brother?[55]

Didn't get to sleep till late because the bunch on the fourth floor were all drunk and raising Cain. It's been bitterly cold here the last few days. Nearly froze going to church this morning.

Just finished reading the sweetest love story – "Fair Game." Also read a historical novel called "The Ugly Duchess" (not so good). "The President's Daughter" that you speak of isn't so much, in fact, not worth your trouble. "The Marriage Bed" and "Oil" (by Upton Sinclair) would both make good reading for you.

Paul Whiteman played at one of the theatres here not so long ago. Most of the fellows were of the opinion that they were rank.

As always, I have carloads of work to do. What we need is a two-month vacation in Florida. How would you like it?

Good musical comedy called "Paris" is playing here on its way to New York. I haven't been able to see it and probably won't.

I'm frightfully sleepy. Can't seem to think of anything more to write about. I hope you won't think this letter too dull.

Love,

John

At this time Terry McGovern was doing considerable traveling in his job with the Missouri Railroad, and on February 27 he was writing from North Little Rock. His letters reflect that he is still frustrated that Jessie is not writing much to him and even threatens to not finish the letter he is writing until he hears from her. Fortunately when he returns home the next evening he is pleased to find a letter, finishes his letter to Jessie and mails it the next day. Terry's regard for Jessie is so evident and we can't help but wonder if she realized his loyalty or if she regarded it as tiresome.

February 28, 1928

Jessie dear,

I'll start this letter to-nite and maybe I'll write some more tomorrow and so on until I get an answer from you to the two notes I have already written. Then I'll mail this. I really am anxious as can be for an answer. I want to know how you are, what you are doing and Oh! a hundred and one things about yourself.

I don't like Arkansas. I hope my sojourn down here will be short. I know it isn't at all sweet.

Regardless of how old it is, I sure would like a picture of some kind of you. Any little "snap" that you have will be quite welcome, and come to think of it, you owe me a picture. Remember your promise?

Right now it's 10:45 pm. Friday and here I am continuing the letter I started last nite.

You know, I'm all happy and excited tonite, for when I came home from work, I found a letter waiting for me, and Oh! it was a nice long one and say, this little Irishman sure was glad to get it. I really didn't expect it before Saturday anyway. So now I'll mail this in the morning. You'll get it Monday morning and, Jettie, if you're nice to me, I'll get an answer next Wednesday.

I hope you'll think I am being nice when I say I'm not going to wait for your answer before writing again, but I will send you another letter before this week-end passes.

You know it was hard for me to know how to write to you, or rather what to write until I got your letter today. I didn't know how you'd feel toward me—but now—I know you're just the same dear old sweet Jettie you always were and I'd give anything to see you right now.

I can think of a lot of places I'd like to be, rather than here and away up at the top of the list is - where Jettie is.

I'm sure I'm not going to stay here so very long. You see this is a good place for me to get some mechanical experience and after I get it, I'm striking out for the North, and by that I mean the United States. This country down here seems almost foreign to me, and I don't like it.

I'm sure sorry, I didn't get to see you at Xmas time, but it really was impossible. You see I went home and worked all the time. I was there in my uncle's store, and I didn't know of anyone who was driving to Clearfield and I didn't have the money to make a trip of that length and since I had to borrow money for carfare to come down here (about $70⁰⁰). I hated to hit the family any harder, so, sweet, you see how it was.

Now, dear, I'll try to make my next letter "neat," as you say. Sweet dreams.

Ever yours,

Terry

Receiving no reply from Jessie, Terry sent the following card to her in March, one of his many hints over the years hoping she would respond:

During these mid-to-latter twenties when Jessie was keenly interested in social events, she could enjoy the fun provided by those able to afford membership in a fraternity. Jessie reveled in this "mad, bad, glad" era of campus life—the fall and spring house party week-ends. While not as much a party girl as those more accustomed to the high life, Jessie could hold her own. Her mother would chide her, "Jessie, every time you come home from a week-end at Penn State your skirts are shorter."

With new machinery and assembly lines, between 1922 and 1929 national production increased by 34 percent, and the consensus among manufacturers was that if it could be produced, it could be sold and a good enough salesman could sell it. Along with aggressive advertising, the 1920s also saw the "canonization" of the salesman as the brightest hope of America[56] and young, ambitious men were recruited into sales (including many of those among Jessie's acquaintances who corresponded with her "from the road").

While these young men received minimum training about the product or service they were selling, the main incentive they were given was sales quotas, setting as the objective for each sales representative as 20 or 25 percent beyond that of the previous year. Contests were devised and large sales conventions were held, gradually becoming more frequent and livelier. At these conventions salesmen (rarely, if ever, women) could learn tricks of salesmanship in an atmosphere of almost religious revivalism with the idea that they would go back to their territories with renewed vigor. With each successive quota number the competition became more intense and, in some cases, cutthroat.

These sales conventions also provided opportunities for the participants to become uninhibited

in their activities in a city where no one knew them.[57] They also often shared the names of young women they had met in their travels and most earmarked towns where public dances were held and where they could meet the local young people. In many small towns where these men were making sales calls the young women found these men interesting company. Most were good dancers, some had had a year or two of college, and nearly all talked a good game.

The following letter was mailed by one such young salesman from Augusta, Ohio, with a return address of Mechanicsville, Iowa; but no legible date.

Jebbie dear –

As for my promise, here it is. I inquired regarding the "special item" I sent you and find it has never been returned here so, that's that. Disappointing, of course, but there will be other opportunities.

Driving over the broad highway today I had quite a long thought – first with myself as I tried very hard to figure a number of things out. First on that list was you – and after an hour or so found I was just where I had started so had to give up, so what a problem child you turned out to be.

I really can't quite see why you will in no way commit yourself – cause if you do just a trifle I can't see where it would do any harm to say so and, after all, it would set my mind a little to rest.

With Love,
Paul

This is another example of probably many more like "Jerry," a salesman whose letter bore no date.

Sweets,

How far is this place away from your hometown and could we get together—John, Leila, you and I for a day together? I don't want to seem selfish, but it would be much sweeter with just you and me. I'd dearly love to see you again even if were only for an hour. Do write and let me know what you think of it. I have every Friday to Monday off.

I hope you won't think of as being bold or too forward in writing some of the things I did in this letter, but, Sweets, that's the way I feel towards you and I can't just say why. So I had better close before I'll be telling things that might not be good for Lovely Women like you to read.

Thanks a lot, Sweet One, for letting me write to you. It has done me a world of good tonight. Hoping this finds you well and happy and that I will hear from you in the near future.

Yours,

Jerry

It may have been one of these letters—or any of the many letters that arrived at 411 Thompson Street—that led Jessie's father to forbid her from dating traveling salesmen. A family story relates an incident in which he would not allow Jessie to leave the house on a date, saying, "They are all the same and I forbid it! I won't have you going out with any horse thieves!!"

While Jessie seems to have enjoyed the diversion of meeting and dating a number of traveling men, she remained more focused on and interested in those she had met through more traditional means, such as summer sessions at Clarion and Penn State and through mutual friends.

John Ditz became the front runner for Jessie's affections in the spring of 1928, although he didn't get home from the University of Pennsylvania as often as Jessie liked. While John's frequent letters were helpful in maintaining her serious relationship with him, Jessie still did not pass up other opportunities to date, nor would any gentlemen of that time have expected her to. Even so, Jessie was not one to keep up her end of any correspondence, a trait revealed through the letters of her many suitors who sometimes kidded her and other times expressed their impatience with her.

March 22, 1928

My dear Jessie,

I thought you said you wouldn't be the first to lag in our agreement in answering each other's letters. What is the trouble now?

John

Jessie evidently responded to this brief letter, offering the excuse that she had been ill. While we can't know if this was the reason she hadn't been writing, John was gentlemanly in his response.

March 28, 1928

Dearest,

I'm really sorry that you have been sick. If only you had let me know I would have written to you every day. Right now, I'm awfully busy, but you know I would do a lot for you.

I'm about as disgusted as can be. It is the same old story—things not breaking right. Another row on with the family. That is constant, though, except that sometimes such as the present it gets worse. Now, of course, I'm in no humor to go home at all. Studied hard for a Business Law exam and then proceeded to get all 5 cases wrong. Worked hard for Industry so as to get a good grade on that exam only to be let down by a lot of trick questions. Such is life—the more you work the less you get.

Monday I have two awfully hard exams and one on Tuesday that is even worse. I never get through.

The last 4 days haven't been inductive to working. Every day the temperature has been up to 75. Mighty nice, of course. Doc and I did a lot of walking. Went out to one of the aviation fields Saturday.

Don't know when I'll get home so it is hard to say just what day I shall see you. I promise you, though, that it will be as soon as possible. Are you going to be very busy around that time? Suppose I phone you from home? Gee, but it _will_ be sweet to be with you again.

Can I beg your forgiveness for the shortness of my note? I'm really sorry; you know I am. I'll try to make up for it. I would write more now, but my nerves seem to be jumpy tonight, at any rate the pen doesn't want to go right.

Please write me a long letter if you are able, darling.

Always, John

While John's difficulty with his classes and exams is surprising because he had been an honor student at Clarion High School and an earlier letter (February 18, 1928) notes that his grades are good, it is evident that he is struggling. From a distance of nearly a century, one still is tempted to say, "You should spend less time at the movies, dances, and the reading of novels and more on the studying." Regardless, John's longing for Jessie is evident from this following letter.

April 1, 1928

Dearest,

I'll try to make this letter better than the last one, but it will be hard for I feel even more blue and disgusted. This vacation can't come a minute too soon for me. Two exams tomorrow and one the next day. Studied yesterday and this afternoon. Now I don't care whether I pass them or not. Just feel like saying, "What's the use?"

I sure would love to have a date with you tonight. That would snap me out of it. What I mean, I'm looking forward a lot to being with you. Are your lips and your kisses as sweet as ever? I hope so for I sure do yearn to kiss you. After all is said and done, you are the only, only one. There is just one you and that's the one I like.

I'm coming home[58] by way of Pittsburgh and I won't get into Clarion probably till Friday night at the earliest. I'm going to hot-foot it over to see you as soon as possible, probably Saturday or at the latest Sunday. If I can, I'll be over early so don't go out till after eight or so and then I'll be sure to find you in the night I come.

I imagine that things aren't going to be so hot at home. Folks are still sore and now I'm getting that way, too. It's a long story. The only answer to it is several million dollars.[59]

Art Connelly has a new car, a Hupmobile.[60] Doc & I are going for a walk to clean our minds. That is a poor substitute for a date with you, darling.

Please forgive this awful letter. I mean well but can't seem to execute it tonight.

Always, John

This time, Jessie evidently responded more quickly than usual.

April 5, 1928

Dearest,

It was so nice of you to write. I had hardly hoped for it. Gee, but it is lonesome here now. Only two other fellows in the dorm besides myself. I'm leaving tomorrow noon [Good Friday] so I suppose they will be left to their lonesome.

It sure is great here tonight. Nice big moon and all—just the ideal night for a date with you, darling. I was thinking tonight that I'm always a fool but sometimes I'm worse—that's when I do things I'm sorry for afterwards. We sure have a lot to make up for lost time, dear. I'm sorry that I even acted as I did.

Didn't do much in classes today as I couldn't find ambition to study yesterday.

I'm glad that it won't be long now till we will be together. Till then I send my love and kisses.

Always,

John

Following Easter at home, which he presumably spent with Jessie since it appears things went well with them, John returned to Penn at the end of the week.

April 12, 1928

Darling,

The first and most important thing today is to write to you. Came in by train this morning. Hap happened to be on the train, too. Punxsutawney had treated him pretty good so he had a lot of news to tell me. Sorry to say I am not feeling overly ambitious; I only went to two out of four classes today. My bad luck is still holding up. Got back another exam with a 65 on it. They say there's a silver lining, so I must be due for a mean run of good luck soon.

The weather is wonderful. Flowers are blooming, shrubbery is green and even the leaves are coming out on the trees. This is ideal for a weekend at the shore; as always though, I'm broke, so that leaves that out.

Hap wanted to go to the ballgame this afternoon, but I couldn't see it. Looks as if the only thing on the program for tonight is a movie and I'm sick of them.

I called you again Wednesday evening from home intending to talk awhile but you weren't in. Looks as though everything we might do together will be all off till summer. I'll probably be home about the middle of June and then we can really get together.

They are still fixing at the car. It's quite a mess. I'm still hoping for a new one by summer. Gee, but I was griped about the other night—wrecking the car didn't peeve me near so much as the knowing that I couldn't get over to see you. I tried to talk Art into getting his car and taking me over but that was all useless. Some people are most darn ungrateful.

[It should be noted that this was close to a two-hour drive.]

Reckon I had better go out to lunch. Drop me a line soon, won't you please, dear?

Love, John

There likely was a response from Jessie, as indicated in the following letter from John.

April 20, 1928

Dearest,

I'm down in Doc's room listening to the radio. He's over in Camden and Charley has gone home. Charley has a real weekend—he goes home Thursday afternoon and comes back Monday morning. I wish you were near so I could do something like that.

As ever, there's work to be done, but who cares? Just finished a book called "Meat" [61] that is supposed to be one of the best sellers. I didn't like it so well. Not nearly as good as Upton Sinclair's "The Jungle." I'll bring it the next time I see you and you can read it and give me your own opinion.

I don't believe I'll bother to refute any of the statements you made in your letter. I think I know the mood you were in. Isn't it awful? I can sympathize with you.

I was going to write you yesterday, but didn't feel in the mood. Right now I doubt that I can do it decently. Guess there is nothing new to tell you. Things drift along as usual. You would think from my letters that I never did any work, but you might be surprised for I really do study a lot. I just revolt against it all so much—I get so sick of never getting through. There is always something to be studied.

Got an invitation from an old friend at Goucher [in Baltimore] to the Prom there, but had to turn it down for several reasons, mostly financially.

I hate to send you a thing like this and call it a letter, but try as I may, I can't write a decent thing tonight. I'm awfully sorry, dear; you really deserve so much more. If you were here perhaps I could make it up, but not so in writing.

Lovingly, With kisses,

John

Jessie's negligence in writing resumed and a stalemate in correspondence between John and Jessie continued for about a month. Finally, John wrote explaining he hadn't written because **she** had not. The information in this letter also indicates that the friendship between John Ditz and Bill Fowler has endured, but that at this time there does not appear to be a serious relationship—if any—between Bill Fowler and Jessie.

May 18, 1928

Jessie dear,

Why didn't you ever answer my last letter? You haven't been ill again, have you? I've been intending to write again right along, but then I got a stubborn streak and put it off, hoping that you would write. You should at least tell me what is the matter. Remember after tears comes laughter.

Went out to Bill Fowler's apartment Wednesday night. We drove up to Norristown. I had called up Tommy [Mary Alice Thompson] and gotten Marjorie Wall's phone number so then I called her up, but she wasn't in. Why haven't you ever written to Mary Alice?

George and I were up to Charley's two week-ends ago. We had a mean time and I got pinched for speeding.

Work has been piling on awful. One exam after another. I have one Monday in Geology that will be awful. Finals are near, too, and I have five of them in a row starting on the Monday following the close of classes on Friday. That means a lot of studying in a little time.

Please write, won't you? I wouldn't ask if I didn't want you to.

Please,

John

Perhaps Jessie's mind was on the coming summer as it was time again for young teachers to make their plans, as to if and where they would be attending college to continue earning their required credits for certification to teach. In May Jessie had three letters from her friend **Zella King** who wanted to room with her wherever they decided to go the summer of 1928.

Punxsutawney, PA

May 20, 1928

...Listen, Old Dear, are you going to school this summer? I wanted to write you sooner so we could room together if possible, for I'm sure we could have a good time, but perhaps you have made other plans by now.

I wanted to go to "State" this year, but suppose I will end up at Clarion. Write and tell me, Jebbie, what you are going to do. I got a school at home this year and I'm certainly glad of it.

I wonder how everyone is in Clarion. Al said Bob had been up to see you several times. I haven't seen any of them.

Write and tell me, Jebbie. I must dress for a date.

Love, Kingie

Five days later, Zella writes again.

May 25, 1928

Dearest Jebbie,

This is just going to be a note as I am going to the movie tonite and must hurry along.

I am so glad we can room together and I will feel lots more like going there, since I will be with you for we can have lots more fun and all that goes with it.

Listen, Jebbie, don't send in your application and we will register like we did last year. I'm going to eat in the Dining Hall, but we will try to stay at the Kissels.

I'm sure most of the kids will try to get down town.

I'm going to write to Mrs. Kissel tomorrow and see if you and I can have the room that you and Al had last year. If we can't, I know a peach of a woman in Clarion and I will try to get there. I am going down next week and I can see about it. I will let you know just as soon as possible.

Al isn't going to school, is she? I haven't seen her to talk with, but I notice she seems quite the same as usual.

Well, Kid, Old Dear, I'll find out and let you know. Remember, you are promised to me.

Loads of Love,

Kingie

In the midst of these decisions regarding summer school, Jessie received the following letter from **Bob Schauwecker** from Dormont, in the South Hills of Pittsburgh, inviting her to a Penn State House Party.

May 25, 1928

Hello, Jebbie,

How's my girl? Thought I'd died, didn't you? Well, I fooled you that time, but I have been busy. We are painting our fraternity house.

Have you as yet decided upon which summer school you will attend? I hope it's Clarion. It's been almost a year since I met you. I started in Clarion last May 21st. Did I tell you I was up to Clarion about a month ago? Well, I was and saw the gang.

Say, Jebbie, Don has asked me to the June house party at State. Can I depend on you to accompany me? We would have an old-

fashioned night as we did last summer at Oak Grove. Well, Jebbie, answer this soon even if it's just a post card, because I want to hear what you are going to do this summer and if you will be able to go to State with me.

Ever,

Bob (Schauwecker)

Plans for Clarion and rooming with Zella were finalized by the end of May, and it appears that at least Zella is looking forward to the summer.

May 31, 1928

Dearest Jebbie,

We are set for the room that you and Al had last year. I like it best for it's large. That's the one I asked her to save for us. Now what shall we do? I'm not going to send my name in for registration because they may make us stay at the dorms, or shall we send in late? What do you think?

Al was talking to Mother Tuesday and told her that you and I would do plenty at Clarion this summer. Wait till I get hold of her! I just hated to think of going to school until I tho't of being with you and now it's not so bad. I hope we have a nice time.

I have bushels to tell you when I see you, Kid, but I couldn't write it all so why start? This pen is a mess, every other word it misses.

Well, Old Dear, write and tell me what you think.

Love,

Kingie

Also near the end of May John Ditz wrote again, still talking about studying, this time for final exams, not an unexpected topic of worry for a student. He mentions two additional concerns, one that he is faced with financial constraints and the other that he evidently had not responded to Jessie's most recent letter in the way she had wanted.

May 29, 1928

My dearest Jessie,

I tried before to answer your letter with apparently no success. It may not be much better this time although I don't know why.

Final exam in English tonight, hence Shakespeare has been my main source of amusement for the last few days.

I'm easily led astray. Regardless of financial embarrassment and lots of work to be covered, I promised to go to Baltimore for the week-end. Now I'm considering the economical side of "bumming" down.[62]

Monday the fun begins so I've started already to try to cram some 380 pages of historical Geology into a lazy brain.

I haven't been doing anything, not even reading much. Worst of all there is no news to tell you.

Till the next time,
Love,

John

A week later John sent the following, the last letter from him that is preserved in Jessie's collection. He apologizes for not responding sooner and plans to see Jessie mid-month in Curwensville. There is a hint of something ominous that he indicates Jessie knows about and we might speculate that the "reading between the lines" refers to conversations they had and more information John provided as to his finances. This also may be the "out" he is giving her in asking if she wants him to stop and see her in Curwensville. On the other hand, his closing gives no indication of anything other than love for his dearest Jessie.

June 4, 1928

My dearest,

When there is the most to be done, I feel the least like doing it. The Geology exam this morning was fierce. Even though it sounds pessimistic, I must say that I doubt passing it. Chances are, though, that I passed the course, at least I hope so. Two tomorrow and one the next day—all tired out already and nothing done for them yet. I'm sorry to have had to postpone answering your letter—You'll forgive, won't you, dear?

The Baltimore trip didn't pan out to be paying dirt. I went down early Sat. morning and came back late that night.

I'll probably be thru your town the 17th or 18th (around there sometime). I'd like to stop and see you. Do you want me to?

This isn't any answer to your nice letter, but you understand how things are just now. Read in between the lines—You'll see that I mean well—.

Love and a million kisses to you.

John

In June the long-suffering, ever-hopeful Terry finally received a letter from Jessie, prompting him to respond with a rambling testament of their friendship and their love—or at least his for her. Ever optimistic regarding Jessie, Terry notes that she asked him to remember that she loved him. We can't help but wonder if this request is based on some separation that occurred between Jessie and John. Terry also responds to Jessie's question as to why he has not written the "kind of letter" she wanted to receive, presumably a descriptive love letter; this might lead us to the same conclusion as to the waning relationship between Jessie and John.

June 12, 1928

M' Baby: --

Which being an expression of utmost affection in the Southland seems to me to be adequately appropriate for the opening of a letter from me to you.

Yesterday afternoon when I returned from my day's labors and found awaiting me a letter from M' Sugar, my joy was unbounded. I experienced that feeling that sets all a person's nerves to quivering with pleasure. The English language is indeed poor in adjectives fitting to describe the joy I felt as I looked at the envelope and received the assurance that it truly was a letter from Jessie.

How hurriedly I tore through the contents of that letter and how rapidly my pulse did beat as the unimagined, even unlooked-for, statements of yours caused the blood to rush through my veins and a flush to begin at my scalp and spread all over my face. And then how slowly I read and reread that letter the letter to digest each and every word in it. How I pored over each word, each syllable, yes even each letter of each word, until I almost knew it by heart.

I read it over and over again and only regret that it

had to come to a close. I do live in hope that your letters will continue to come, so that I may know again a little of the old joy that I once experienced from your letters and from your love.

As you say, school will soon be out. Have you any plans for the rest of the summer? Surely you expect to take some vacation. Where will it be spent and how? If only we could be together for a few days - Oh! wouldn't that be nice? However, that's impossible.

You used to ask me why I didn't write you the kind of letter you wanted to receive. Can I be frank with you? Well, then, here goes. A fellow doesn't care to have his correspondence to any girl become public reading matter. Not that I think my letters to you ever would be that, but perhaps I was a little afraid that you might read to, or allow to be read by your chums, some of my letters. Personally I want your letters for my eyes only and I'd like to think of my being treated likewise. <u>Can't you give me the assurance that such will be the case?</u>

Precious, in your letter you asked me to remember that you loved me. If that be so, Honey, sure you can scare up some sort of picture to send me. One that is less than five years old for that is the latest one I have from you and though it's cute and I couldn't be tempted to part with it, I'd enjoy having one of more recent date. Can't you send me one <u>now</u> that more nearly pictures you as you are today?

Then, too, sweetheart, you might tell me something of yourself, are you the same doll I once loved so tenderly and are you the same girl, the memory of whom occupies a place in my heart no other can touch? Or are you perhaps completely changed, a stranger to me?

Tell me about all your beaux, your dates, what are they like? What is your favorite liquor? Are you dancing much and where? Oh! Jessie, there are a million and one things I'd like to hear from you, all about you, Babe.

Personally I have changed a lot. I believe I'm getting old. I haven't been to five dances in five months. I enjoy a good time as much as anyone, but I believe that along with all that I've accumulated a lot of good common sense. I may have had a half dozen dates since the time I came here. I'm not sure. However, I know there haven't been anymore than that.

I started to write to you last nite, but I was so sleepy I gave up and went to bed. The weather here has been so hot that it is next to impossible to sleep. Still I'd much rather have this weather than Winter.

Now, Doll, I'll close for my eyes are growing heavy.

Lovingly,

Terry

P.S. Please enclose the picture in your answer to this—soon.

It must have been crushing for Terry not to have received a reply to this effusive letter. He has poured out his heart after seemingly receiving encouragement from Jessie and an expression of her love for him.

We can only imagine what Terry must have thought not to have heard from Jessie—rebuffed, slighted, foolish, or angry. Lesser gentlemen would have not written to Jessie again, at least until they had received a letter of apology or an explanation from her. Terry tries in the following letter to rationalize what might have happened that Jessie has not written to him. However, his perplexity is palpable.

Terry evidently wrote several other letters to Jessie between the one above of June 12 and the one below of June 28. Jessie did not answer any of them.

The letter which follows here was sent to Curwensville and then forwarded to 113 Becht Hall, Clarion Normal School, where Jessie no doubt was enjoying another summer as a co-ed. One has to wonder if Jessie was vacillating because, after receiving Terry's heart-pouring letter of June 12, she (1) decided her affections were not for him, (2) was being courted by others who held her interest, or (3) simply procrastinated as was her habit. In any case, it is painful to read Terry's utter defeat, albeit a defeat beautifully expressed offering to settle for only friendship if that is all Jessie wants.

June 27, 1928

Jessie, dear,

If receiving a letter from me is distasteful to you, I ask your forgiveness, but you see from time to time little things occur that cause thoughts of you, all of them called to arise in my mind. It seems that whether or not I so desire, I cannot entirely control my thoughts where you are concerned. It is impossible to completely eradicate memories of you that are constantly recurring to me.

Often have I wondered whether my failure to get an answer to several of my last letters was of your own choice or perchance that of your parents.[63]

Be that as it may, herein lies another attempt on my part to renew again that correspondence which in days gone by, kept alive in both of us closeness and friendship, or mayhap it were more true to use an expression, conveying a feeling, more deep, more strong, and more amorous.

It would cause me much pain and unhappiness were I convinced you cared naught for letters from me. To me, all of your letters have ever been dear, more than welcome, and always have they caused those pleasurable little thrills of joy to chase each other up and down my spine. They always have bought a flush of joy to my cheek, and a throb of ecstasy to my temples.

Perhaps my letters bored you, caused you no little thrill of anticipatory joy, were rather an undesirable element in your otherwise happy existence. If such be the case 'twere for better that we should never again hope to hear from one another. That we should never look forward with a pleasant thrill of anticipation, to that time, when we shall again see each other.

I do look forward to again meeting you somewhere, somehow, and of searching again the depths of those twinkling, lustrous eyes, in the hope of finding there perhaps some small spark of feeling that shall kindle and burst into flame with that same strong emotion that was rooted so deeply in both of us.

Yes, I meant rooted so deeply in both of us that possibly it never can be entirely extricated, but shall like the germination of wild plant life reproduce itself time after time on down through the years to come, until that day when death shall have beckoned to the last of we two, and we shall have answered. After that, who knows?

It would indeed be a shame if such a friendship as ours should die for want of cultivation. The cultivation of correspondence, a letter now and then requires but such a little bit of one's time.

Perhaps you remember, dear, and I may call you dear, may I not, for you will in truth be ever dear to me, perhaps only in memory, but nevertheless, dear, what ages ago I asked you to consider me always, your very best friend. One to whom you could bring your troubles and confidences, and sorrows, and be ever sure of finding a willing ear to listen, and to console and maybe to advise you. You never have availed yourself of that privilege, if I may presume to call it a privilege.

'Tis needless for you to tell me that you have never, in all that time wished for someone in whom you could confide. Would that it were so, but life is not like that. Ah! Jessie, that hurts a little for I know that you must have had occasion to long for such a friend and yet you utterly forgot old "Terry." I wish it weren't so.

I suffer now that your school year is ended you are back again at Clarion. If that be so, I'm sure you are having a wonderful time and I'm glad, for I like to think of you as having a good time.

Well, Jessie, all good things must end, even this letter, so before closing, in case you do not desire to correspond with me, at any rate please at least send me a card and say so. If I don't hear at all from you I'll not know for sure whether you are in "this vale of tears."

Forever,

Terry

Just when it all seemed to be finished between Jessie and Terry, he received a letter from her three weeks later on Friday, July 20. Whatever she wrote must have erased all the anguish he had felt in writing the above letter of despair. Terry notes that he had made several attempts to answer her letter of July 20 before completing it on July 23. How vulnerable a position he is now willing to place himself in as he pours out his heart, ranging from humor, then relief and most certainly to writing the kind of love letter Jessie earlier had requested. He writes to Jessie at Clarion from his boarding house in North Little Rock, Arkansas, using his usual fine quality stationery.

July 23, 1928

M' Baby,

Since you like that term, and since it so fittingly describes the way I feel, I again so open my letter.

Could you but realize how hot it is in this room and what a task the heat makes letter writing, you'd surely feel as if I must care quite a bit or I'd not be writing at all. This is the third time that I have begun a letter to you, M' Sweet, since I received your precious epistle Friday. This "oven" has kept me from completing either of the other two, though I really tried to answer your letter promptly. Were it not so insufferably warm, I'd sit me down here and print an answer so that you could read what I'm trying to say. As it is, I'll just write this and hope you can make a little sense out of it.

Picture me here, if you can. I'm sitting in one rocking chair, with my feet in another, before a window wide open, clothed only in "shorts" and trunks. I'm almost melting. My entire body is covered with perspiration, and in order to keep it off this letter, I have a blotter under my hand that I keep sliding back and forth across the page.

Baby M' Love, I was simply delirious with delight at your letter. I've read it over and over until I almost know it by heart. That one remark of yours about the "driven snow" and not having "drifted either" was rather clever. However, if I cared less about you, I'd ask you if you ever noticed how dirty nice white snow gets after it has laid in one place awhile?

Again, Hon, I ask you to excuse the appearance of this letter. My position is not at present the best possible for letter writing and is not at all the one I usually assume.

Could I but have that one kiss you said you'd give me, and then you said, too, that you'd make me love you and sing you to sleep. Would that I were but there to love you. But sing you to sleep. Never? Evidently you never have heard me sing. I alone am the one person with a musical sense strong enough to realize the beauty in my vocal endeavors. When I sing it is either in the privacy of my own room, in the bathroom, in a crowd, or when I want to torment someone. Never to give anyone pleasure. And that is that.

You spoke of my loving you. Don't you think I do? If you were here now, it would be but a matter of a very few minutes until you were convinced of it.

How deeply your kisses are burned into my lips. Even now I can still feel the joyous pain of their exquisite fervor. Never will their sweet ardor be dimmed by the haze with which passing years are wont to diminish past happenings. Rather will their sweetness be enhanced and live forever within me, burning my lips, as glowing coals of passion when as is frequently the case, in my memory I live again those joyous days of yesteryear.

Could I but have you with me for one short hour, I know you'd never have to ask me again, "Do you love me?"

Jessie, dear, tell me honestly, are your letters as sincere as I want to believe them? I hate to ask this question, but Darling, please don't feel hurt. I must know.

Love forever, Jerry

Terry writes again, revealing quite unexpected information based on the passionate tone of his letter to Jessie three days earlier.

Terry McGovern

M' Baby Sweetheart,

I am so happy, dear, to have a response from you so quickly! I hope this means I no longer am going to have to worry every day about not hearing from you and to figure a way to cajole you into writing to me.

First, let me respond to what you wrote. You say I'm not changed at all. Babe, you are mistaken. You'd be surprised at what an utterly changed person I am. Really, dear, I'm just the most old-fashioned person I know. All my gallivanting around has made of me just the most sincere home lover imaginable.

I ask for nothing better, can really think of nothing finer than to sit on my own porch in the cool of the evening, with the girl of my dreams, and, who knows, perhaps also a wee babe to brighten our lives. Really, dear, I hope you can see just how domestic I've become, for I'd hate to give you a wrong impression. However, I also enjoy a good time as well as ever I did. But, I'm more sensible now than ever I was, so I don't live entirely for a dance now and then.

Perhaps some nite here I'll step out and have me a date. There really is one girl here I could enjoy a date with. Her name is Marie Pyle. I like her a lot now, and that is one reason why I hesitate about having a date with her. I don't want to cease liking her.

In another letter I asked you if we couldn't be perfectly frank with each other. To show I meant that, here goes.

You no doubt are wondering about another Marie since I had told you about that first Marie many years ago. I am sure you remember that I said at that time how big a mistake you and I might have made had we ever gotten married. Of course, we might not have, but it did make me realize that regardless of my love for you—which is stronger than I have ever felt for anyone else, I don't think I could marry someone who is not Catholic. Probably one of the happiest moments of my life was on that Xmas morning when I was able to go to church and to Communion with Marie.

If it had been you and I, you would have been going to one church and I to another, and although our love might have been great enough to overcome that, still it wouldn't have been at all pleasant.

You also spoke of hoping that you never would have a baby and asked my views on the subject. Jessie, that is a subject that is very dear, almost sacred to me. Lord, but I love kids. I hope God will be kind to me and give me some of my own someday. Does that express my views clear enough to give you some idea of how I feel on the subject?

Well, Jessie, Sweet, regardless of what I say now, I do still love you, or rather I love the girl I used to know. I love Marie Pyle, too. I'd marry her right this minute if it were possible. There are several things to prevent it. What they are I won't bother to explain. At the time when you receive this letter she will be in Europe. She left on July 20 on Knute Rockne's Olympic Tour, and will get back in September.[64]

It's a queer predicament to know that you love two girls at once. I never did expect that to happen to me.

Now, dear, do you appreciate my frankness? Is it going to make any difference in your letters to me? I do hope not, and I also hope you'll be equally frank with me. Who's your best sweetheart? Tell me about him. I'll look for an early answer. I mean immediate and if you but enclose your addresses in Altoona, Canton and DuBois, and tell me when you will be there, I'll see that you get letters there.

Admiringly, Terry

While Terry could not yet have had a response from Jessie on his revelation that while he loves her he also loves another, he began another letter to her the same day. However, the postmark reveals that this letter was not mailed until July 31. Somewhat inexplicably, Terry himself remains exhilarated in this letter, seemingly without worry that he has confessed his love for Marie Pyle in addition to his addressing Jessie as "My Own."

The **last section** of the letter below is written following Terry's receiving a card from Jessie. It is likely that she had received the above letter; perhaps learning of the competition for Terry's affections made him more attractive in her eyes, or perhaps she was relieved that she did not have to commit exclusively to Terry, or maybe both Terry and Jessie simply realized that regardless of their feelings for each other, their religions would be a barrier. It also needs to be considered that the tempo of the times, as well as Jessie's own personality, promoted popular young adults enjoying multiple "beaux" or "belles."

Wednesday (July 25)

My Own: --

God, I take a lot for granted. Still, regardless of whatever does happen to either of us, somehow that feeling will persist always.

Did you ever stop to think, isn't love a funny thing. Here I am some 1100 odd miles from you, dear heart, and yet the mere thought of you sends a pleasant, painful shrill all over me.

What's that-you can't understand that painful. Lord, Jessie, don't you suppose it pains me not to be able to see you.

How I wish I could again hold you - Oh! so tightly, and whisper to you sweet nothings, what yet carry a world of affection, adoration, and soundless love. The love of a little Yiddish boy for a little Swede girl. Oh! Excuse me, I made a mistake. I meant my love for you.

The Lord only knows why I am sitting here now writing this since I have already mailed one letter to you tonite, and yet I know I could go on and on and on writing to you and never feel tired. I must care considerably for my Jessie. If you remember—"Jessie" is mine. I originated it, and still it lives even as my love lives.

Hon, I know I'll not send this for a couple of days and since I must write to my brother tonite, I'll put this aside until.

———

Here it is Friday now. I mean Saturday. And say, Sugar, you've no idea how much real satisfaction I got out of the card I received from you today. Can you imagine why? I'll tell you.

You know it would have been quite easy for you to have been kidding me along in the letters you wrote, but somehow or other just your card asking why I hadn't written seems to tell me that my letters really do mean something to you. I hope they do because, "My Own," I really do mean for them to mean a lot to you.

Last nite another fellow and I rode out to Fair Park. There we listened to a dance orchestra play two numbers and Gee! It sure did make me want to dance. I had felt that all desire to dance was gone from me, but I guess it never will be.

I'm not going to mail this letter until I get an answer to the two I have already written, and when I do get your letter which will no doubt be Tuesday I'll finish this pronto and dash to the P. O. with it. Now I guess I'll go down to visit a young married couple here in N. L. Park. We might have a game of Bridge before the night is over. For the present, then, my love, adios.

The tide, however, shifts once again when Terry receives a letter from Jessie, very possibly Monday which is the day he responds. The content of her letter appears to be very upsetting to him. He returns her letter. (Unfortunately, the letter Jessie sent him and that he returned in this envelope with his long response and demand for answers was not found among the letters in the trunk.)

Monday (July 30)

(Terry's style of handwriting changes here to a larger sprawl, perhaps an indication of his anger and haste to reply)

Jessie,

Just got home from work, and received the enclosed. You can have it back. I don't want it. If you have to write letters like that, don't bother to write at all. Now I suppose I won't get any answer to this letter, but I'd rather get none at all than the kind I received today.

I wish you'd look over the letter you sent me that I am enclosing and see where I have underscored it. Dammit, Jessie, I _do_ love you.

Your Terry

P.S. If _that_ means anything to you

In addition to his underscoring parts of Jessie's letter and returning it, he also then added the following comments in the margins throughout and around his own letter:

1. *Why don't you enclose your DuBois and Altoona and Canton addresses. I want an answer now.*
2. *I'm waiting for an answer.*
3. *Are you going to answer this today? You'd better.*
4. *P. S. More later – Please answer pronto.*

Tucked into this same envelope is a message written on note paper:

6:30 p.m. Just finished eating my supper and now before I mail this: I love you, I love you. It's all that I can say, etc., etc. I'm glad as I can be that love picked out a little boy like me for my Sweetheart.

We are left to guess what happened between Jessie and Terry at this intense point in their uneven relationship. There is no way to know if there were letters that are missing from the collection in the steamer trunk—although most of the letters in the collection are sequential and connected. The next evidence of Terry in Jessie's life doesn't occur until almost a year later.

While we also have no way of knowing the extent of Jessie's heartbreak—or not, nonetheless, there were always new men to meet and more fun to have, in addition to the arrival of fall and another school year. The young adults were all too willing to follow the suggestions made in the current popular tune "Makin' Whoopee."

Just like clockwork the Sixty-fifth Annual Session of the Clearfield County Teachers' Institute was held in the Clearfield High School Auditorium in August 1928. Attendance was required even though the only program section of interest to Jessie Pifer was the listing of all teachers in Clearfield County. Two names, in addition to her own, are marked with a handwritten check mark – Philip Mannino, Madera, Smoke Run Intermediate School and John Stodart, Madera, Manor Hill Grammar School. John must have been of special significance, for his name in his own handwriting also appears on the back cover of Jessie's bound program.

Some Sunny Day

Judith Thompson

By
Irving Berlin

Irving Berlin, Inc.
MUSIC PUBLISHERS
1607 Broadway   New York

O n the national scene, Herbert Hoover had been elected president in the fall of 1928, but when President Hoover was inaugurated on a cold, chilly day in March 1929, the ingredients for a global recession were gathering. The literature of the period also portended a darker period with Hemingway's *A Farewell to Arms,* Remarque's *All Quiet on the Western Front,* and Wolfe's *Look Homeward, Angel,* all three books darkly brooding. In contrast, the best songs of the year were the lilting "Singin' in the Rain" and "Tiptoe Through the Tulips," but both were eclipsed by "Stardust," the most popular song every written.

Silent films had run their course, as the public stopped attending any movies that didn't have sound. Also during this year the first motion pictures in color were exhibited by George Eastman and color television was demonstrated as a possibility, indications of the greatness to come in leisure activities for Americans. What caught the public's imagination, however, was the concept and then construction of the world's tallest building, the Empire State Building.

Commercial aviation, more popular in Europe, was slow to get under way in the United States, but the public's interest in flying was heightened by Colonel Lindbergh's transatlantic flight and landing in Paris. In celebration Curwensville High School's Class of 1928, as well as other schools throughout the United States, wrote the name of their yearbook in French. Soon the terminology of flying found its way into everyday use such as in this letter written to Jessie in 1929 by one who would play a key role in her life:

"Yes, I just made a non-stop flight, landing at 12:45. Sure did burn up the road, from Uniontown to Morgantown and back home."

1929 brought into Jessie's life two new suitors, Harry "Doc" Hawes (from Cherry Tree) and Russell Stuchell (from Indiana, Pennsylvania) who was working in Detroit. Stuchell and Hawes evidently had met Jessie and joined the long line of her gentlemen callers who, despite all odds, still included the perennial Terry McGovern.

The first of these new gentlemen to write to Jessie was Russell who seems to be assuming that Jessie is making a trip to Detroit.

January 12, 1929, Detroit, Michigan

My Dear "Jebbie,"

Well, I suppose you believe that I have forgotten all about you by this time, but such isn't the case. I have been so busy seeing the town that I haven't done much of anything else.

I am not settled as yet and with such a place I have to write on, I certainly hope that you will excuse this awful writing. Also, I must have left my fountain pen in Curwensville, because I can't find it any place. The last I remember of it was in the Curwensville National Bank last Saturday evening at seven o'clock. I went to use it and it was dry and I must have left it there.

My cousin and another fellow and I left Indiana at 12:20 a.m. Sunday and arrived here Sunday afternoon at 3:30. Pretty good for a Ford coupe, considering that we stopped quite a few times en route.

There is going to be a bridge party here at the house and my cousin and I are invited. I sure am a good bridge player. I guess I have played the game about three times total.

I hope that everything is fine in Curwensville. I haven't looked up any of the boys from there as yet, but will as soon as I get settled. It was hard to leave Curwensville when I was just getting acquainted real nicely like I was when I left.

I am real sorry that I was so bashful and didn't make your acquaintance before. Maybe we can see more of each other this summer when you come out. Let's hope so.

This place has changed quite a bit since I was here before. There are some wonderful new buildings and theatres here. We took in the new "Fisher"[65] last nite. It is certainly the most wonderful place I was ever in. The show wasn't so hot, but the place is.

Well, must close now and get ready for the card party. If you were here I sure would show you the town. I'll be looking for you this summer. Don't forget now, and please write real soon. The address at the head of this letter will reach me for the present.

Sincerely,

R. W. Stuchell", Russ" or "Doc"

A month later Russell writes again.

February 11, 1929

Dear Jebbie,

Yes, dear, I did receive your letter and I know that something terrible should be done to me for not answering sooner.

I am working now in the day time, and when you come here, I think you can see how easy it is to put off writing at nite. I am getting bawled out from all sides, both family and friends, for not writing. When I get back to earth and settled down a little I know I'll have more time to myself.

A friend and I went to look up Blake Korb (from Curwensville) and "Jing" Johnson the other nite. We found Blake but not Jing. I also saw "Rusty" Way. I didn't know him so well.

I had a letter from Doc Yurmann the other day and I'll have to get busy and answer it one of these days, too. Say, if I sat down and wrote all the letters that I should, it would take me from now on.

Don't think for a minute that I didn't write because I didn't feel that way, cause that wouldn't be the truth. The next time I'll answer just as soon as possible.

I hope that you and the rest of Curwensville are as fine as ever. I should drop Doc Crissey a few lines too, and will one of these days. He sure is a fine fellow. I don't know what I would have done there if it had not been for him. I know what I should have done, though, and that is make your acquaintance sooner.

Now, be sweet and write and don't do like I did in delaying to write.

Sincerely,
Doc (Russ)

In typical Jessie fashion, it was a month before she responded to Russ. And like most of the young men with whom she corresponded, he was very pleased to hear from her regardless of the delay. As often happened where Jessie was involved, Russ indicates that Jessie has made plans to go to Detroit for a visit with him during the summer of 1929.

March 14, 1929

Dear Jebbie,

Well, at last the long-looked-for letter came. I thought that you had forgotten me altogether. When I waited so long to write before, and you wrote to see what was wrong, I thought that after I did write, you would answer right back. (Say, before I go any farther I want to ask you to please excuse this pen.)

So you think that I didn't miss your letter. Well, I did, and was trying to figure out why you didn't write. Well, I believe you made me wait nearly as long as I did you.

I'll bet you are glad that you only have two and a half more months of school. Then you will be coming to Detroit, won't you? So you have a new dance hall, eh? Well, maybe I could dance there if the lights are dim. Say, that was a good story you wrote me. Where did you say that hotel was? Why did she have to be on the floor, anyway?

No, it will be impossible for me to get home for Easter, no matter how much I would like to. If I go home, it will be later in the summer. I have been thinking all along that you will be out here this summer. I don't know why you believe that I didn't want to be bothered with you at Curwensville. You think that because I was (or am) a little bashful, that I didn't want to be bothered. Well, you are wrong. I wanted a date with you more than I did with any other girl in Curwensville. "Soupy" Hipps [also from Curwensville] kept saying that we would date you and Kate Smith some nite, but that nite never came. Anyway, he said you were his girl and I would have to go with Kate.

Say, do you think you would like me with a mustache? Well, I have a pretty good beginning of one, and I like it myself. I believe you would, too. It might jag a little, but you wouldn't mind that, would you?

Jebbie, I hope you get this on Saturday because I don't want you to have to wait until Monday. I'm sorry I can't tell you a story, but mine are all too bad. I forget so many too. I hear plenty, but can't remember them. Please excuse this writing, it is terrible and I'll try and do better next time. I'll say good-nite now and sweet dreams. Be sure and write and soon.

With love and kisses, Russ

Three weeks later, Russ wrote again to Jessie after she had replied to his March letter telling him that she would not be going to Detroit in the summer as they had assumed. Because Russ would not be able to get to Curwensville until September, chances were slim that this relationship would continue.

April 8, 1929

Dear Jebbie,

Well, here I am again, late as usual. I suppose you have been looking for a letter each day since Easter. My intentions were good, but I just couldn't get around to it. I wrote my first letter in over a week yesterday and that was to Mother and Dad. I am starting to get caught up again tonite.

You said my last letter was adorable. Well, listen, if I could write letters half as nice as you, I would think I was wonderful. Sorry you had to make so many starts the last time. And say, who said your letters appeared dumb. Anyone who said a thing like that ought to be crowned. I can't even remember of getting any letters than were more lovely than yours.

Am glad you like moustaches. Say! Is it moustache or mustache or what have we? I guess I have been spelling it wrong. I haven't one of those loud hats[66] yet, but have been thinking of getting one. Just to show you that I am not trying to please the girls, I won't get it.

I am real sorry to learn that you won't be in our lovely city this summer. I thought that Kate's boyfriend was here in Detroit and that was why you were planning on coming. I don't expect to be in Pa. until September. I sure would like to be there sooner, but don't see how it can be done. We had some wonderful days here last week. Just like June. We had a fine drive yesterday to Ann Arbor. We drove all around the University and the large stadium and just had a wonderful drive. We were plenty warm in our shirt sleeves. It turned colder today again. I suppose the weather there is about the same as here.

When I get a good snapshot of myself and moustache I'll send it to you. Don't hold your breath waiting for it, tho, 'cause I take very few good pictures. I don't know just how many cameras I have ruined.

Haven't been to any shows lately. Saw "The Carnation Kid" a couple of weeks ago. It wasn't bad for that kind of a picture.

Say, watch yourself at the Golden Wedding Anniversary 'cause I wouldn't want you to get oiled and no one to take care of you.

Must close now, dear, and write two more letters before I go to bed.

With love and kisses, Russ

Jebbie and co-ed friends

Detroit was barely thought of again with Summer Sessions offered by the Pennsylvania State College beginning the second week of June. Penn State's education extension courses for college credit were held at convenient locations throughout the state, including Clearfield, "wherever twenty or more students gathered."[67]

Nonetheless, Jessie, ever the co-ed even at the age of twenty-four, preferred to be on a college campus. She was familiar with Penn State as she had attended a number of fraternity house parties through friends of Bubby Thompson when dates were "imported" and resided with their chaperones at one or more temporarily vacated fraternity houses or boardinghouses. There were five on-campus fraternity houses in the 1920s at Penn State and Jessie loved these former mansions that suggested the glory and glamour of an earlier age, to say nothing of the wealth of the previous owners.

The summer of 1929, where nary a whisper of the impending Depression was heard, Jessie roomed at the Phi Sigma Kappa fraternity, converted for the summer to a campus boarding house for women. Jessie loved telling her friends that she was staying at a fraternity for the summer—and not explaining any further unless pressed. She took two courses, History 18 and Sociology 2, for a total of six credits. The classes each met for eighty minutes a day, five days a week, for six weeks, which tied up more than half of her day and half of her summer. One can only speculate that she fully partook of campus life as she did not fare well in her courses. Perhaps the lure of a larger, more sophisticated college was too attractive to resist, although historically Penn State during that time is said to have been much "tamer" than many of the other colleges.

Some afternoons Jessie took the train to Altoona where she visited her married sister Josephine, occasionally staying two days and missing her classes. Even at age 24 Jessie requested of her older sister, "There's no need to tell Mama I am missing my afternoon class. I'll make it up later." Evidently she did at least hold her own, as the standard Penn State transcript reports her grades of "2" (good) for History and "0" (passing) for Sociology, in the unusual grading system of -2, -1, 0, 1, 2, 3.

In some ways, the trends for nearly all young people caught up to what Jessie and some others had already been doing. For example, in the early 1920s Jessie had applied Tangee lipstick in the mornings on her way to high school (so her parents would not know), but it wasn't until the late 1920s that the vogue of both rouge and lipstick spread swiftly to the smallest villages. It is estimated that by the end of the decade three-quarters of a million dollars was being spent by American women on cosmetics and beauty shops. In the June 1929 issue of *Ladies Home Journal* (which a decade earlier had refused to advertise cosmetics) there appeared a lipstick advertisement with the comment, "It's comforting to know that the alluring note of scarlet will stay with you for hours." [68]

Neal Buchanan, who had first met Jessie in 1927 after which they had a falling out, re-entered the scene less than two years after the break-up. Using B.R. Cummings Co. stationery Neal writes from DuBois with some trepidation, almost as if he is being interviewed as to whether or not Jessie will see him.

June 26, 1929

My dear Jebbie: --

I don't know whether this letter will find favor with you or not. It is not arriving at the time promised, and "dear girlie," I will not try to offer any lame or absurd excuses for its delay. However, in order that you might know I have been thinking about you, this is the third attempt at writing this letter. So no matter whether right or wrong, thoughts are conveyed to you as you may believe. I am trying to make this a good ambassador from the poor correspondent.

It is much easier for me, dear, to do many other things than to write a letter in which you are to judge whether I may see you again. Somehow I feel that this is going to prove a failure for I do not know just what you will expect. However, it is my best and comes from my heart without any reservations. I have not called you on the phone, because I knew that this letter must be written. I do hope, Jebbie, that this short note will be favorable to you and that soon I may see you. I would like to say much more, dear, but am afraid as to how it may be taken. However, I am waiting anxiously to hear from you and to know that I have not altogether failed.

Love,
Neal

Jessie evidently replied favorably to this letter and Neal Buchanan was back in the running. Receiving her letter at noon, he responded immediately and with enthusiasm from the Acorn Club of DuBois, a popular social club of which he was a member.

July 2, 1929

My dear Jebbie,

Please forgive the hurried writing as I would like for you to receive this before the 4th. Found your letter this noon, dear, and was mighty glad to hear from you. Last Sunday evening I talked to Walt at the Sweet Shop and he told me you had left for State College. I am sorry, dear, that my letter was not written sooner; then perhaps you might have permitted me to see you before leaving. The best I can hope for is that you will allow me to come over when home for a holiday or to arrange an evening at State College as you suggested. You can always find me, Jebbie, at either my club or home every evening, so don't fail to give me a ring on the phone should you drop in to Curwensville unexpected.

No doubt it is great to be at State during the summer term, and I am glad to know you are furthering your education there. Oft times I wish that my school days were before me, for after all, they are the best days to live.

Don't study too hard, dear, and whenever you can drop me a line as to what you are doing, please do. Your letter will be answered promptly and every bit of news that might interest you I will send. Even tho my letters seem dull to me, honey, I will never forget how good they were to receive while away at school.

I hope you receive this before the 4th and that soon I may hear from you.

Lovingly,

Neal

It is likely that Jessie spent the Fourth of July with Neal. However, Jessie also apparently met Harry Hawes somewhere along the line during the hiatus with Neal. The following letter does not appear to be Hawes's first to Jessie; however, it is the first letter of his that Jessie kept. Hawes's home was in Cherry Tree, near Indiana, Pennsylvania, and some thirty miles from Curwensville; thus, Jessie and he likely met through mutual friends or at one of the several public dance halls in the area. The fact that he is suggesting that two couples rent a cottage near Philipsburg the following week-end is a strong indication that Jessie and he have been dating seriously. Harry, known by most people as "Doc," was to play an important part in the life of Jessie Pifer and here he is writing in response to a letter from her.

July 5, 1929 — The Big City, Friday Night

Dear Jebbie,

Yes, dear. Just a little late probably about three days, but you know the old excuse, very busy. Your little letter was very much appreciated, but by my not answering you probably think it wasn't. However, the big rush for the 4th of July sure had me stepping. Spent most of the day in bed, played golf, and had a swim. I didn't have enough ambition to go to Sunset (Ballroom) or Ebensburg last night.

My trip to Pittsburgh last night was not so good. I had called Don about two from home, but they said he was out so I played golf until five thirty and then started the drive to Pittsburgh. The traffic was so heavy I didn't get there until ten thirty. I then called him on Monday night but didn't get to see him as I was busy. Turns out he was coming home on Tuesday to a family reunion at the farm. Red is working with Don, so it was just like old home week all day. They sure do make a good pair. I also had a letter from Tom who wants to be remembered to all of the gang.

Tuesday night I went to the dance at Ebensburg with Dick McLaughlin. We were with girls from Glen Campbell. Dick can get a cottage down by Philipsburg any week-end if it would be alright with all concerned. How about the week-end of the 13th? He will be here on Tuesday of next week; I think you would like his girl—she works in the bank with Ted. If you would rather not go on a blind cottage date with another couple don't hesitate to tell me but I really think you would like them.

Dear, I didn't like that statement in your letter about me probably not taking your picture out of the car. You know me better than that. The picture of you has a permanent place on my dresser and I am telling you now it is going to stay there. It seems just like a member of the family—couldn't get along with out it.

Just had a call from a fellow in Spangler. He sold a big commercial Frigidaire today. They are going over to pick it up but it sure does take work.

It's about time I was coming to a close or you probably will be late from a class if you read this all at one time. I don't know if there are any questions in your letter I haven't discussed. As I don't have it here in front of me I don't know. However, I do remember the apology you had at the beginning (Was that necessary?) and the little way in which you called me down for not asking you to write.

Yes, and about our date last Saturday, dear, I never will forget it. When I think of it I just wish you were here for just a few minutes of loving. See, isn't it wonderful to love when it means so much?

Please leave me know if you want to go on that cottage week-end.

Your Sweety,

Doc

On July 8 Doc mailed a letter he had written on July 6 to Jessie in State College confirming plans for the couples' cottage week-end and telling her how much he is looking forward to it.

July 6, 1929

Dear Jessie,

Right now is just the time on this Saturday night that I should be leaving for Curwensville, but instead I am spending the night at home for a change.

The family asked me this evening where I was going to spend the week-end and when I said at home they wanted to know if I was sick.

I was in Glen Campbell today and talked to Ted. We are having a big game of golf at 10 a.m. if we both get up that early. Have been getting up early all week as my sister is home with the boys and they don't believe in anyone sleeping late. Her boys sure are bricks; they have the house and yard looking the same as it did when I was a kid building trains with furniture etc.

It sure does seem a long time since last Saturday but I am just looking forward to next week-end. Hope all the plans pass with your approval.

Must say good-night as this is just a note.

As ever,
Doc

The following day the ever-faithful Terry sent Jessie a birthday card from Fond du Lac, Wisconsin sent from "ISHIPEMINC & CHI R.P.O."[69] to Curwensville; it was then forwarded to Jessie at the Phi Sigma Kappa house in State College, postmarked July 9 from Curwensville.

Meanwhile, Neal wrote to make plans to go to State College to be with Jessie for the week-end following the couples' cottage week-end (when Jessie would be with Doc Hawes).

THINKING OF YOU

A little greeting
Just to say
I'll think of you
On your birthday

Terry

July 9, 1929

Dear Jebbie,

I realize this letter should have been written days ago, but there has been so much for me to do the last few days that I simply could not concentrate on what I wish to say to you. It was lovely, hon, to hear from you so readily and even tho you will not believe me, I appreciate it a lot.

We are starting a sale this week and the next there is scheduled a big celebration for the opening of the Du Bois Air Mail Port. I am going to write you a letter and send it by the first Air Mail out of Du Bois. Stamp collectors have already offered one and a quarter dollars for these envelopes. So you see they are well worth keeping as a souvenir. Then, too, I hope it is the only one to State College and my little "honey bunch" will have the honor of owning it.

I should have written Sunday, dear, but for the fact that a very good friend[70] visited me the entire day and evening. He drove from Birmingham, Alabama and it has been nine long years since we saw each other. He is the assistant Rector of the Episcopal

Church in that city. Naturally we used up all spare time talking about school days.

I believe, dear, that a week from this coming Sunday I will be able to come over to State. If this is all right, hon, may I come over early and spend the entire day with you. You see, my Dad is on his vacation and this will be the nearest day I can set in order to see you. However, should there be an opportunity of getting over sooner I will let you know in plenty of time. Until then, sweetheart, don't forget me or my

Love,

Neal

Jessie received the following mail on July 9, her 23rd birthday: a telegram from Helen and Peg, a birthday card and letter from Kate Smith, a letter from Helen Decker, and a postcard from Mary Alice Thompson sent from a New Jersey resort.

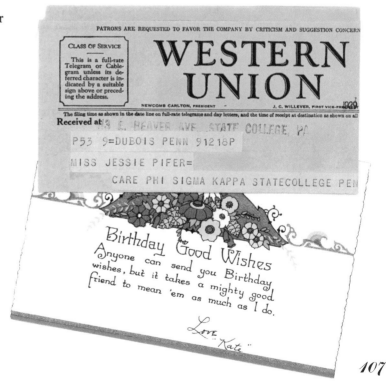

PATRONS ARE REQUESTED TO FAVOR THE COMPANY BY CRITICISM AND SUGGESTION CONCERN

CLASS OF SERVICE

This is a full-rate Telegram or Cablegram unless its deferred character is indicated by a suitable sign above or preceding the address.

WESTERN UNION

NEWCOMB CARLTON, PRESIDENT   J. C. WILLEVER, FIRST VICE-PRES

The filing time as shown in the date line on full-rate telegrams and day letters, and the time of receipt at destination as shown on all

Received at 3 E. BEAVER AVE. STATE COLLEGE, PA

P53 9=DUBOIS PENN 91218P

MISS JESSIE PIFER=

CARE PHI SIGMA KAPPA STATECOLLEGE PEN

Birthday Good Wishes

Anyone can send you Birthday wishes, but it takes a mighty good friend to mean 'em as much as I do.

Love
"Kate"

CONVENTION HALL AND SOLARIUM, CAPE MAY. N. J.

Alcott House, Cape May, N J [71]

Dear Jessie,

*This is the place where we dance. Haven't met anyone exciting yet.
Have been working quite hard. Where are you going to school? Write.
How is Doc? And also my boyfriend?*

Love,

Tommy (Mary Alice Thompson)

Dear Jebbie,

Did the whole house collect around your door when you got a telegram? We hoped they would. We'll surely have to come again because of what we forgot last time. We forgot to pack the dinner buckets to hang on the doors. I'll truly bring them the next time if the Phi Sigs continue to dress so for dinner. That I can't do down in my linen dress. I wished then that I had brought the pails right along.

I can just see and hear you saying "Listen to this, she spells college with a "d" in it, honest to God, right here it is."

We sort of think we'll come down week-end after next if that's all right with you and if it isn't, we'll come anyway. How about it?

Kate had a headache last night so she didn't come down town. I took Blanche, Gretchen Leib, and Mother to see "Show Boat" (wealthy, don't you know). I liked it very much.

Diz never comes around any more. If that's the way she feels about it, I should worry. Well, Jebbie, do write soon and leave us know the news and don't study too much.

Hel.

Dearest Jebbie:

Better late than never—I surely am ashamed of myself for not writing sooner, but I just coun't bring myself to it—too hot—anyway, honey. I want to thank you for the lovely time you showed me last weekend.

We had quite a trip home—I think we laughed most of the time. We came home by way of Snow Shoe and it surely was a pretty drive and just at that time in the evening. We stopped several times along the way but made good time. As usual I missed a date with Norman—Mother said he called twice. Hell!!!

Last night Diz and I went to see Corinne Griffith in "Prisoners"[72] —not so good and I was bored to tears. I was just dying to go to the dance, but there just wasn't anyone to go with me. Chet said they had a wonderful crowd—just loads of strangers—I asked if Dely was there but couldn't find out—that brat of a Norman might have asked me but I guess he has called his last.

Have you had any cute dates? And oh! How I crave a good necking. I sure could give someone a good "going-over."

Well, Jebbie, dear, must stop my rambling and get dressed. Yes, I still have my long hair—just haven't the nerve to cut it. "Be Good" and don't do anything I wouldn't do—(right now I could do most anything though). Write and tell me all the news of the "college," all about your dates 'n' everything.

Heaps of Love,

Kate

Of more import than college dates and hair cuts during those times, however, is that by 1929 close to a million investors were buying on margin—putting up only a fraction of the price of the stocks they bought and a million or two citizens were following the financial pages. Everyone, regardless of their lack of real understanding, was speculating—housewives, ranchers, clergymen, doormen, and whoever else could put their hands on some cash, did. One such naïve investor was Neal Buchanan.

July 10, 1929

Dear Jebbie,

I didn't mention this in my letter yesterday but the last few days I have been buying stock on the New York market and have put myself in the box to the tune of a thousand dollars. However, by a little careful saving on my part this will soon be straightened out. I don't know why I tell you this, dear, unless it is that I feel sure you are a good pal and will forgive me for thinking about stocks when I had a letter of yours to answer.

I think of you constantly and look forward to seeing you very soon.

Love,

Neal

What most people did not realize is that the speculative market had become so huge that the mechanisms that were supposed to make it self-regulatory would become mechanisms for compounding the catastrophic results. Once the downward spiral started, there would be nothing and no one to stop the rush toward economic disaster.

The next day Jessie received a letter from Doc Hawes with the disappointing news that the couple's cottage plan for the coming week-end was off.

July 11, 1929

Just a short note. Received your letter this a.m. In regards to the week-end Dick is going to New York, so all plans concerning him is off, but I still will be down Saturday probably 4 or 5 p.m. Will try and make it in time for dinner. If I can't, I will call you Saturday at noon.

Will be seeing you,

Doc

Amidst all of this romancing from Neal and Doc, Jessie wrote a letter to reliable Terry. Evidently Terry and Jessie had not been corresponding. He notes that when he was home (now in DuBois) during December Jessie had not kept much in contact with him so he was surprised to receive this recent letter from her. Terry wanted her to know that he had had to borrow money to take a job offer from American Telephone and Telegraph Company (AT&T) in Chicago, and since then had been traveling in this job. He writes on July 13, 1929 from the Calumet Hotel,[73] Fond du Lac, Wisconsin.

July 13, 1929

Dear Jessie,

Whoever said that the 13th wasn't my day? I know it is because I got a letter from you today. And Oh! Boy, I sure was glad to get it.

I guess I do owe you an explanation about last Christmas time, Jessie, and now I'll give it to you frankly, honestly, and without any excuses of any sort for myself. For one thing I didn't get many letters from you while I was home, but that didn't keep me away.

As you know I got home from Arkansas in poor health and very much in debt. I don't suppose you knew about the debts, but you did know I was sick. I was home about two months and didn't work at all. All the money I spent during that time I got from my folks. Then they wouldn't even think of letting me go back to Little Rock to work as I had to hunt a new job.

During my quest of a job I made a trip to Hagerstown, MD.[74] (No, I'm not married.) That cost the folks another hundred, so I couldn't with a clear conscience ask them for money to make any pleasure trips, especially after landing a job with the A.T.& T. Company in Chicago and having to borrow money enough to take it.

Please don't think, Jettie, that I didn't want to see you because I did and I still do and you can't imagine the thrill I got out of your letter today. Now to get on with the story. I went to Chicago Feb. 10 and took a job with a crew of locators. My first stop was Gary, Indiana. We were there until late in April, and when we moved up here about a month ago I got a crew of my own and now have five fellows working for me. Ordinarily I would have only two, but this is a rush job. I got a ten dollar a month raise in pay and a lot of compliments on my work so I think I rate pretty well.

However I'm working like hell. Night and day. I can't even keep my correspondence up, so the fact that you are getting such a prompt answer from me should give you a slight inkling of what I think of you, Jettie.

Physically I feel fine, though I'm having a little trouble with my teeth. I've been going to the dentist daily and I have an appointment for 7:00 pm. tonight and this Saturday. Socially there's sure a fine gang of girls here that we've been rushing pretty strong and I'm having a peach of a time.

Now, Jettie, dear, I've got to close, take a bath, shave, dress, eat, go to the dentist, and then have a date, so won't you excuse me, Hon?

Please answer this promptly because I may be pulled out of here any time after Wednesday. I'll leave a forwarding address in case I do. Perhaps next time I write I won't be so loaded with work and I'll be able to send you a respectable letter.

Your Terrence

It is fairly evident why Jessie didn't respond to Terry at all, let alone with enthusiasm. Not only did Terry mention he was going out on a date later that evening, but also Jessie was too involved with Doc Hawes, whose letter she received a few days after hearing from Terry, to think much about Terry.

July 18, 1929

Dear Jessie,

I just got home from another little trip. I was down near Edith's home. Went down to Uniontown on Tuesday then on to Morgantown on Wednesday. Came home this morning so you see how I have been sleeping.

Dear, sure did enjoy the week-end with you; certainly had a wonderful time. How a little loving from someone you love sticks in your mind. Just can't forget that loving we had Saturday night. Wasn't it wonderful, dear?

How did Edith and Kenny get along? He seemed to like her. Hope we can have the Sunday together we planned.

Must close and get this on the 4 o'clock mail so you won't think you have been neglected.

Your Sweety,

Doc

Letters from Kate Smith and Helen Decker in late July are here included because they provide a glimpse of letters written by Jessie's contemporaries since we do not have any of Jessie's own letters. The second letter references the postponed couples' cottage date.

July 22, 1929

Honey,

I ask you – what shall I say, for God knows nothing ever happens here.

Just came home from town. Helen has a date with Fred Staver (Do you remember him?) so Blanche and Gretchen are playing bridge with them. God! I don't know what I would do on a date it has been so long. By the way – Peg Forcey introduced Helen and Fred and they are just getting along famously.

Coming home next week-end? I'm getting homesick to see you, so trot along. I have just oodles to tell you about Bill. We had a darling time – suppose Louise told you. And, oh!, his line, but believe me, I think I have fallen or if not, have stumbled very hard. Can't decide about letting him come back. We were out for breakfast and then at Bilger's Rocks for about three hours. Just wait and see!!

We had a very nice time at Libby King's bridge party – I won second prize – a vanity [75] similar to the one Bill gave me only without lipstick. Getting good, eh?

Glad you and Doc had such a nice week-end. Has Dely been over yet? I haven't seen a thing of him. Irene Sykes is having bridge tomorrow nite – thought maybe I would go over to the dance but can't now. My good-looking cousin (the one from Pittsburgh) is coming down and I just guess I won't get to go. He is the one we should call when in Pgh.

Percy dear was here last nite but as I went to bed with the sick headache about 8:00, I didn't see him. He was telling about Ted Stauffer getting married. Quite a shock to everyone. Just wonder what Tommy [Mary Alice Thompson] thinks.

Supposed to have a date with Norman Wednesday nite but gee, there isn't a single thing to do. He is sort of cute, tho.

Well, girl friend, [76] I can't manage this pen any longer so must hit the hay. "Be Good" and if you haven't anything on for the week-end, come home.

Love,

Kate

July 23, 1929

Dear Jebbie,

  I do hope you will not mind this paper, but if I didn't write here at school you'd not have the pleasure of hearing from me. Right now I'm helping Dad with some books that have to be gotten out by Thurs. so it keeps me humping to do my shorthand, keep gadding, and do my work at the office, and also my washing and whatnot.

  Last Fri. noon I went home with Peg to Reynoldsville. That night two men from town took us to that camp near Brookville I was telling you about. We had a few liquids, then played the Vic ^{77} and danced. The fellows then made a fire and made sandwiches and coffee. We rolled home about 2:00. The next nite (Sat.) the same two took us to a party a young couple was having at their home. Another good time was had. Sun nite Hoddie and Fred Staver came over. We played bridge for awhile and then, oh, you know, just played around. Last nite I thought I'd get a bit of sleep but Fred called and asked if I didn't want to see the show at the Lyric. I said No, that I wasn't dressed. He came up anyway. Tonite is Club at Irene's so I'm hoping to lose some weight by losing sleep.

  I haven't seen hide nor hair of your Deelee [Dely] since a week ago Fri. when we were going over to meet the kids at Osceola. He was in the ball field at Clearfield but didn't see me. Bless his heart!

  Did the kids tell you about the drunk man we had so much fun with that nite coming from Osceola? That night

Hoddie, Peg, Fred and I went to Anchor Inn. It's pretty nice out there, isn't it? Ha!

Aren't you coming home with the kids? We ought to scrape something up for Sat. nite. How about it? I have a date Thurs. nite with Fred so probably won't on Sat. but maybe we could do things? I suppose you and Doc did things and saw plenty week before last. Kate told me what you kids did.

Have you heard about Ted Stauffer marrying that girl from Delaware, I think? Pretty sudden-like. Your mother called me over last nite and gave me some delicious homemade buns. They were awful good. See you soon?

Love, Hel.

A month passed between a previous letter from long-suffering Terry and this one. He is still at the Calumet in Wisconsin and, as usual, concerned that he hasn't had a letter from Jessie.

August 14, 1927

Dear Jessie,

Just a note, my dear. You see some time ago I got a letter from you, in which you mentioned receiving a birthday card from me. That letter came from Penn State, and I did answer it promptly. That's been some time ago and since then I haven't heard from you at all. Of course, I'm curious. That isn't like you so I want to know whether you ever got the letter I sent to State. Did you? I'd like to hear from you, Jessie, and whether you care to continue a correspondence with me or not.

Please answer this.

Yours, Terry

After an absence of perhaps two-and-a-half months, Neal also re-appeared on the scene following a telephone call to Jessie three days prior to writing his letter. He addresses the situation that they had not seen each other for some time and wonders whether or not she even wants to see him again. He writes from the Acorn Club.

September 20, 1929

My dear Jebbie,

Just a short note to explain why I called Tuesday evening. Some of my fraternity brothers were throwing a supper on Wed. evening and I thought that you might have been persuaded by yours truly to go along. I had to go to some small towns near Curwensville that evening and not leaving much spare time I asked Tom to tell you I had called. Every likely he did not see you as I understand there was a dance there. However, the next time I will make sure that I am notified in plenty of time so as to ask you along. This was the first time girls were ever invited and it was a huge success.

I am sorry that we have not been able to see each other for so many weeks, Jebbie, and sometimes I have wondered whether you want to see me or not. I realize that at times my attitude has been somewhat crude, but really I don't mean it to be.

Perhaps before the snow falls, you may see fit for me to come over. There is nothing more or less to it, Jebbie, but that I would like to come to see you providing that you are willing that I should.

Well, hon, I must close and get to bed for tomorrow is Sat. and a hard day ahead.

Write to me soon.

Lovingly,

Neal

P.S. The club is doing a prosperous business these cold evenings.

Two weeks later Neal wrote again, after Jessie and he had a date. More importantly, after thanking Jessie for the nice time they had, he expresses that he hopes when they speak later in the week that she will tell him he may come back to her.

October 8, 1929

My dear Jebbie,

This is just a short note, honey bunch, to let you know that it will be impossible for me to call you Wed. Eve. At 7 o'clock as we had planned. Thursday evening starts our bridge contests at the club and since I have had the honor to be elected to the entertainment committee, it is imperative that I be there for the start of the series.

Therefore I am writing to you today to see if I may call you Thursday evening at 7 o'clock and learn whether I may see you Friday evening or Sunday at anytime or all times.

I certainly want to thank you, hon, for the nice time last Sunday and I hope that you will tell me Thursday evening when we talk that I may come back to you.

Don't forget, honey, that I love you.

Lovingly,

Neal

P.S. Excuse this pen as it is the best I could find at the store. Don't forget Thursday evening at 7 o'clock, dear.

Sadly, this is the final letter from Neal.

Nothing could have prepared Americans for what was to come and the majority of them spent the summer of 1929 enjoying events that never again after this time would be taken for granted. Historians later called the summer of 1929 America's Indian summer. However, once the crash started in September, there would be nothing and no one to stop the rush toward economic disaster.

Early in September the stock market began to crack. It quickly recovered only to fall again, rise, and fall yet again until on the morning of October 24, it broke wide open. The leading bankers of New York met to form a buying pool to support the market and for a few days there was a rally. Nonetheless, it soon became obvious that nothing could stem the tide of potential disaster. Telephone lines clogged, the ticker was running late. Within hours the Stock Exchange's whole system for the recording of current prices and for communicating orders was unable to cope with the emergency.

On October 28 the US Stock Exchange collapsed and US securities lost $26 billion in value. Then on Tuesday, October 29, the storm broke with full force when over sixteen million shares of stock were thrown on the market by frantic sellers. John Kenneth Galbraith called it, "the most devastating day in the history of the New York stock market and it may have been the most devastating day in the history of markets."[78] It was not until more than two weeks later on November 13 that order was restored.

Most people in Curwensville weren't paying close attention to the event of order being restored to the stock market that day, as November 12 and 13, 1929 were the dates of the town's annual musical production. The Opera House was filled for the two-night run of "Spanish Moon," as everyone in town knew someone in the cast. Lead roles were played by Joseph Hipps, among others. Jessie had a featured role as Valera, billed as a Spanish vamp. Jessie loved the part because it was exotic; she was well cast in the role. Evelyn Williams Milligan recalls the show with fondness and some amusement, "None of us could dance very well."

The winter of 1929-1930 provided a brief intermission in the country's history, with top executives in both government and business reassuring the nation that the recession was only temporary and that the worst was over. However, they were to be proven very wrong.

Looking back on the 1920s, historians note this time as the decade when women gained their freedom—freedom to work and to play without the trammels that had bound them heretofore to a life of comparative inactivity. Yet Jessie Pifer seems to have been born expecting freedom. She had always lived by her own rules—not at the expense of others, but simply by who she was. She was never rebellious; she was just living her own life. She was a responsible citizen and a good daughter, and she had not brought any embarrassment to herself or to her family. She held what might be called a "good" job for a woman, certainly a profession with high respectability in a small town. Thus with a new decade on the cusp, Jessie Beverly Pifer looked forward to all life might yet offer.

Little Girl
Words & Music by
MADELINE HYDE
and
FRANCIS HENRY
OLMAN
MUSIC CORPORATION

The 1930s

Early in 1930 a "wait and see" attitude concerning the economy prevailed and many of the events of the year were not at all reflective of the terrible times yet to come. Rather, there was an odd sense of "normalcy," an interlude from worry with only occasional flashes of concern.

In 1930 the new pastime of miniature golf was introduced with great success in Florida and was followed the next year by the installation of driving ranges for golfers. Golf itself had been increasing in popularity among those of the young, middle class, particularly after Bobby Jones's quadruple triumph, at the age of 28, in the British Amateur, British Open, U. S. Open, and the U. S. Amateur.

The inexpensive pastime of contract bridge also gained more popularity, but among a different crowd and for a different reason. In private homes playing bridge cost little (refreshments) or nothing to play and many pastors no longer decried against card playing—or at least against contract bridge, rationalizing that it was more a game of intellect than of chance. In truth, many of the clergy didn't want to take away one of the few free pastimes parishioners could enjoy.

Chicago, Ill.,
May 23, 1930.

Dear Gibbie:

This is the third letter I've started to you. The last I've torn up because — well because they seemed too much like love letters for me to send to a married woman.

I don't think it's at all improper for me to write this letter to you even though you are married, for surely I'm going to be allowed to offer my congratulations, and maybe sing my "Swan Song."

I only received your announcement a few hours ago at the office and I must confess it really was quite a shock to me. I was affected by it a lot more than I like to admit even to myself.

To be quite truthful I must admit that my plans for my vacation this summer included a stop of several days in Curwensville, and who knows maybe I even had hopes of affecting a reconciliation. That's the reason I was so anxious to re-establish correspondence with you. I wanted to make sure I'd be taking my vacation while you were at home.

Well it's too late now to think about that any more so we may as well get on to something else.

The scene with Terry Mc Govern and Jessie Pifer continued with the same score and in spring of 1930 Terry is singing his familiar song of pleading to Jessie to write to him. He sends her a card from Princeton, Illinois.

Three days later he mails a note card from Chicago with the same theme, not yet knowing why Jessie has been silent.

Terry had no indication that the beautiful Jessie Beverly had eloped! Jessie had called her sister Kate on a Friday evening from Greenville, the seat of Mercer County, saying, "I'm on my way to Mercer to be married at the Justice of the Peace."

As Jessie's sister Kate remembers the event,

"Where? Who?" Kate asked. "Jessie, what are you talking about? Why are you in Mercer County? That's practically to Ohio. I thought you were going to visit Ruby. How did you get there? We thought you were taking the train to Canton. And what do you know about this man?"

"Don't say 'this man,'" Jessie said, an edge to her voice. "You know who he is, Kate."

"Well, yes, but not very well," Kate agreed.

"Just do me a favor and go up and tell Mama, won't you? I would call her if she had a phone."

"But, what will I say?" Kate pleaded.

"Tell her I am getting married this evening and that I'll see her Sunday night. Doc will drop me off on his way to Harrisburg. I'll see you sometime next week."

"What about school?" asked Kate.

Jessie replied, "Well, if you would be a dear and also teach for me Tuesday and Wednesday, I can go with Harry to Williamsport. (Kate had already offered to teach on Monday for Jessie, thinking she would be taking the train from Canton to Curwensville on Monday.) Would you do that, Kate? It would be so nice to be able to take a little wedding trip. I know you said you would teach for me on Monday so I could stay an extra day at Ruby's, so it would just be a couple more days. You aren't working at the Sweet Shoppe until Thursday, are you? Please, Kate? I could stop and see Mama on our way to Harrisburg and pick up some other clothes."

"Then when you get here you can tell her yourself that you got married, can't you?" asked Kate. "I don't know what she'll say. I know she'll be disappointed that you didn't tell her what you planned to do."

"Kate, I have to go. Will you do this for me?"

What could Kate say but, "Yes."

Mr. and Mrs. John Pifer

announce the marriage of their daughter

Jessie Beverly

to

Mr. Harry Benjamin Haines

on

Friday, the twenty-first of March

Nineteen hundred and thirty

at

Mercer, Pennsylvania

Several weeks later Terry McGovern, along with other friends of Jessie, received the announcement of Jessie's marriage.

Stunned, heartbroken, and then resigned, Terry remained controlled and respectful of Jessie's choice, Always a gentleman, Terry closes by reminding Jessie that he remains her best friend.

May 23, 1730

Dear Jessie,

This is the third letter I've started to you. The rest I've torn up because - well, because they seemed too much like love letters for me to send to a married woman.

I don't think it's at all improper for me to write this letter to you even though you are married, for surely I'm going to be allowed to offer my congratulations, and maybe sing my "Swan Song." I only received your announcement a few hours ago at the office and I must confess it really was quite a shock to me. I was affected by it a lot more than I like to admit even to myself.

To be quite truthful I must admit that my plans for my vacation this summer included a stop of several days in Curwensville and who knows maybe I even had hopes of affecting a reconciliation. That's the reason I was so anxious to re-establish correspondence with you. I wanted to make sure I'd be taking my vacation while you were at home.

Well, it's too late now to think about that any more so we may as well get on to something else. I want you to know that you have all my best wishes and if your marriage has given your husband as much pleasure as it has given me sorrow - why, then, Jessie, he loves you a lot so be as nice to him as you want him to be to you.

You know, somehow the idea always seemed to linger that some day things would all turn out all right and that we'd be-well, anyway, I've always had a sort of feeling that we really were meant for each other. Now I just can't seem to realize that you actually are married and that any dreams I may have had must fade away into the land of "Never - can - be."

I know that even though another has won your heart, I still have your friendship and I'd like to repeat what I wrote in a letter to you long, long ago. "I want you to feel that I'm your very best friend and that any time you ever have need of a friend or a confidant, little old Jerry is more than willing to serve in any way he possibly can. Please don't ever hesitate to call on me any time I can ever be of any assistance whatever."

To your husband I extend my most sincere congratulations and a confession of chagrin. I'm very anxious to meet him and to enjoy his friendship as well as yours. (Maybe you all will extend an invitation to dinner sometime - I'll accept, too.) As long as I'm writing I may as well make a letter of this for though I do expect an answer to this. I don't even dare hope for any future letters from you-other than cards at Xmas and on my birthday.

Is old John Wright still in Curwensville? How is he? And Alice Wall, is she still there? Is she married? Gee, I'd like to see all the old gang again.

As for me, this is the news. As you know I'm working for the American Telephone and Telegraph Co. I've got a pretty good job and very bright prospects, good health. I'm having a lot of fun and I'm even managing to save money-for the first *time in my life.*

At present I'm working in the office here in Chicago. However, I expect soon to be out in the field again up around Northwestern Wisconsin. Still the office will forward your answer to me in case I'm not here so send it along and I'll not bother you any more.

I think I had better close this now though I could go on and on, but I mustn't let myself forget that you're married. Please remember, I am your best friend.

Wishing you all the happiness in the world, I am

Always just —Terry

P.S. I know you don't expect it, but on your birthday I'm going to send you some little wedding gift for your new home.

Terry's letter above is one of the three most memorable letters in the set, despite its being written on lined notebook paper. This choice of paper is so unlike the Terry we have come to know that we must wonder if, because this is his third attempt at a response, he likely had run out of his fine stationery.

When Jessie returned to Curwensville she discovered that even her lifelong friend Joe Errigo was as surprised as everyone else at the news of her marriage. He, of course, was too much of a gentleman to ask her why she had decided as she did. He was also somewhat preoccupied in the flurry of opening his own drug store which he called The City Drug Store. It opened April 30, 1930 and Joe didn't see Jessie until she stopped in his store in mid-May.

As Joe remembers that day, he greeted her, "Mrs. Hawes, welcome! You have broken all our hearts." Jessie laughed, but did not respond.

After school closed in May (she finished the term), Jessie moved with her husband to his home town of Cherry Tree. The practice of hiring only unmarried women had relaxed, but teaching jobs were not easy to find in the shadow of a pending national Depression, and Jessie was having difficulty finding a position in or around Cherry Tree. She wasn't too worried about working, however. As she told her mother, "I have a husband to take care of me."

That summer, like many brides, Jessie shopped for silverware at Marshall Field and Company in Pittsburgh. An invoice provides a glimpse of both the cost and the way silverware was counted by the dozen and fractions of that dozen. The invoice for her silver was sent to Mr. Boyd W. Hawes. Later a check with Jessie's signature indicates that this was her own purchase and not a wedding gift. The list also shows that even a person of modest means was interested in having the "proper" table setting. One, however, must wonder how often such a home would have need for a sugar shell spoon, let alone a pickle or an olive spoon.

2/3 doz Rogers Silver	1/12 gravy ladle	1/12 dessert server
2/3 fork	1/12 butter knife	1/6 table spoons
1 1/3 t-spoon	2/3 butter spreaders	1/12 salad dressing ladle
2/3 salad fork	1/12 sugar shell	1/12 olive spoon
2/3 bouill spoons	1/12 pickle fork	

Total $51.57 (no tax)

Harry Hawes promised Jessie a good life with him, a house, travel, nice clothes, and status. He had big plans to open his own store, perhaps in Huntingdon. The kind of life Doc offered appealed to the adventurous Jessie and she was happy to spend most of the summer just enjoying her new station as a married woman. As she wasn't keen on spending time in Cherry Tree with nothing to do, occasionally she went on the sales trips with her husband. She soon tired of that, however, as there was nothing for her to do while Harry was calling on clients or delivering merchandise.

In the midst of this adjustment to her life we find a reminder of Jessie's long-standing habit of lateness or even neglect in responding to mail when she received a letter, dated August 21, 1930, from the School Employees Retirement Board reminding Jessie that she had not replied to their request of June 2 for her married name and that they could not process her request until they had that information in hand.

Before too many weeks had passed, Jessie began to think about her decision to marry Harry Hawes, particular during the days when he was on the road. First, she reasoned, she had been bored with her life in Curwensville. Her social life had begun to slow down and she attributed this to several reasons, although she had not set them in her mind in any order: (1) none of her friends had any extra money to spend on social activities, (2) an increasing number of her friends were marrying, and (3) she didn't belong to the Country Club which more and more was becoming the only spot in town for recreational and social events.

A possible fourth reason is that Jessie may have been noticing that magazines were beginning to extol marriage and family life, even though hundreds of thousands of young people who wanted to get married could not afford to. The marriage rate per thousand population was falling, from 10.14 in 1929 until it would reach a low of 7.87 in 1932.[78]

Nonetheless, marriage seemed to have become more highly prized as an institution, and according to a survey conducted by *Fortune* magazine, "Sixty per cent of the college girls and fifty per cent of the men would like to get married within a year or two of graduation." [79] Many college administrators were said to have noted that college girls of the nineteen-thirties were more eager for early marriage than those of the nineteen-twenties. According to some observers, the Depression seemed to have made some of them more respectful of a "meal ticket" and of security. [80]

Jessie continued to hold strong hopes of finding a teaching position in Indiana County, as it did not look like Doc was going to get his business established as quickly as he had hoped with the economy in such a slump. She did work part-time in the Hawes' family Clover Farm grocery store but she did not much like that work. Doc's income was not as great as it had been the first nine months of their marriage because of the Depression and his clients simply did not have the money to buy anything except necessities; in addition, a number of the grocery stores he serviced faced losing their businesses completely. A list found among his letters indicates at least part of his itinerary.

Worse, Harry had hinted that if things did not soon improve financially, the young couple would have to move in with his parents. This did not please Jessie at all. "If I wanted to live with someone's parents, I would have stayed home," Jessie wailed. "I miss my friends, you are always on the road, and this town is even smaller than Curwensville."

True to form, Terry mailed a first anniversary card to Mrs. H.B. Hawes in Cherry Tree to make sure she received it by the anniversary date of March 21. We are left to wonder if the slight to Mr. Hawes was intentional or that maybe Terry couldn't bear to include him in the greeting or felt he didn't need to since he had never met Mr. Hawes. As is typical with Terry, the card is of the best quality.

The tailspin of the economy that had begun in the summer of 1931 continued until mid-1932 when nearly 12 million people—about 25 percent of the workforce—were unemployed. Soup kitchens and breadlines became common in the cities, and shanty towns began to spring up. Jessie could not find a teaching position in Cherry Tree and she told her mother that she would be coming home to find a job.

Two weeks later Jessie arrived by the New York Central Railroad [the main line from Cherry Tree], with luggage and other odd boxes. As she stepped off the train, she was glad to find Mr. Korb, the familiar drayer who would transport her heavier items. Even so, this was a mixed blessing as Jessie realized that he would quickly spread the word that Jessie Pifer seemed to be returning with all her belongings. "Good," Jessie would have thought. "That will save me the trouble of explaining."

She hoped she would not run into her father before seeing her mother, and was relieved to find that his drilling machine was not in sight as she neared the house. Entering through the back door as was the custom for family members, she greeted her mother who had been pondering for days about what she would say upon her daughter's arrival. Her response was clear in both tone and meaning, "Welcome home, Jessie."

Jessie was hopeful that she would be assigned to a school, for she was beginning to feel the pinch of not having her own money to purchase a few stylish dresses. The length of hemlines was dropping again (and daytime dresses would drop to within nine to twelve inches from the floor by 1933),[82] and Jessie could lengthen her hems only a little as the hems didn't have enough fabric to be let down to the fashionable length. Dress styles also were changing and Jessie didn't sew well enough to be able to redesign her dresses by adding ruffles, bows, and other embellishments. To make matters worse for one who had very little sewing skill in tailoring, waistlines of the thirties dresses had returned to their natural place.

Thwarted in her attempts to re-invent her wardrobe, Jessie decided she at least could let her hair grow since the short, shingled style was fading in popularity; nevertheless, she also knew to have it look its best required a good haircut to even the length. She bemoaned that she didn't have the 50 cents required for a decent cut and she couldn't bring herself to ask her mother for the money when she wasn't able at the time even to pay board. With her world turned upside down, Jessie was disquieted. "This is not the way things were supposed to be," she said to her sister Kate. The assumptions of her world had failed.

Near the end of August she was offered a school to begin the 1931-1932 school term at the salary she had held since she had begun teaching in 1924. She did not hesitate to accept.

Tuesday

Dear
Just a note to say
I wont be up tomorrow
Fritz is going to C.T.
and I am staying at
the Store Kate
going away Thur
so I'm going to
but Isy will
Saturday come
Clearfield or
bus so I'll try
be in
Eig

Wednesday
5 P.M.

Dearest
Just had a
interview with mr wright
am going to work at
once we are leaving at
7 P.M. for Baltimore
to by a truck of Produce
will be back some time
tomorrow. Sorry Dear
but I wont get to
this week
be over on
about 3 P m
want me to
drive over in
morning. that is
going to take
it. If any
should happen
would half to
I will call.

All my
love
Dan

"The Reliable Hotel"

THE LEISTER HOUSE
HUNTINGDON, PA.
W. H. McClelland, Prop.

Darling
I have a interview
with a mr Wright at 5 P M he
is opening up a market
here on Friday of this
week. Talked to his
today but didnt have
time to go over everything
as he was going to Baltimore
to by produce today
will be over on
Thursday if nothing
else comes up.
All my love
Dan

Tuesday 8 P.M.

Dearest
Just a note am going to see Crawford & Gabel in 6 rained tonight. Didn't here anything from N.Y. since Sun. probley will tomorrow Forgot last night to tell you about the big strike in the silk mill hue last week. will tell you Sunday.
This closing at 6 gives me a chance to get caught up in my movies.

last night I worked and tonight don't have a thing to do. Sure wish you were hue It seames so long thease whole weeks do hope we get settled soon. I wish now you had come over and we were going to the dance tonight But we will soon be togather.
All my Love
Doc.

Monday 10 P.M.
Darling Just finished with the inventory & the weeks profit. Dear I sure did miss you over the weekend. It seames so long since we were togather. There is a good dance at Altoona tomorrow. Sure would like to take you. But N.Y. conclusion is so bad I expect bad news any minit.

All my Love.
Doc.

will be waiting for my letter.

Records indicate that Jessie remained in Curwensville. Harry evidently corresponded with Jessie and visited her in Curwensville with some regularity. However, the next available letter is four years after their marriage. In 1934 he was working out of Huntingdon and relates what sounds like a house move for his parents. His family ran a Clover Farm store, but it appears he himself was not working there, but continuing in his sales position. He opens the letter with an endearment.

May 2, 1934

Dearest,

Just finished a real day's work. It sure is a dirty job. If I ever get in another job of moving I think I will go nuts.

Got home Saturday night. I packed all day Sunday. The truck came in early on Monday morning at 5 and left at 12:30. I came down last night. I like the new house fine.

I expect to go to Williamsport on Thursday and come back on Friday by way of Lewistown and get Mother. Sally may come up along.

Dear, I will drive over on Sunday afternoon. It sure is lonesome. Wish we were together tonight so we could enjoy the moon.

Do not know any more news. Will be seeing you.

All my love,

Doc

Fewer then two weeks later, Harry again writes from Huntingdon using an envelope with the return address of Hawes Clover Farm Store, Cherry Tree. However, he has crossed out everything except the name HAWES. We might surmise that the separation of Jessie and Harry continued to be caused by the lack of work because of the Depression. There is no definite indication of any other reason based on the love expressed in the letters.

May 15, 1934

Dear,

Just a note to say I won't be up tomorrow. Fritz is going to Detroit and I am staying at the store. Kate is going away Thursday and Friday so I am going to be busy. I will see you Saturday. Come to Clearfield on the 7:00 bus and I will try to be in before eight.

All my love, Doc

Three weeks later Harry writes from the Leister House in Huntingdon where he apparently is living; this indicates that he is living alone and not with his parents.

June 6, 1934

Darling,

I have an interview with a Mr. Wright tomorrow at 5 p.m. He is opening up a market here on Friday of this week. Talked to him today but didn't have time to go over everything as he was going to Baltimore to buy produce today. Will be over on Thursday if nothing else comes up.

All my love, Doc

Later in the same day, Harry sends Jessie a second letter with good news.

June 6, 1934

Dearest,

I just had an interview with Mr. Wright. I am going to work at once. We are leaving at 7:00 p.m. for Baltimore to buy a truck of produce. Will be back some time tomorrow.

Sorry, Dear, that I won't get to see you this week, but will be over on Sunday at about 3 p.m. or, if you want me to, I could drive over in the morning, that is if we are going to take lunch out. If any thing should happen that I would have to work I will call.

All My Love,
Doc

It is September before Harry writes again. Perhaps he was seeing Jessie regularly enough that letters were not necessary. What is evident, however, is that Jessie is in Curwensville when schools are back in session in the fall, adding to our knowledge that she and her husband still were not residing together.

This new school term (1934–1935) found Jessie in a rural school at Bridgeport where she would remain for the next decade. Bridgeport School, in Pike Township, was perched atop a hill above the Crescent Division of North American Refractories Company. Jessie greatly wanted to purchase an automobile since there was no public transportation to the school, two and a half miles from her family's home on Thompson Street; however, she did not have enough money. There had been no salary increases since she had begun teaching ten years earlier, and as late as 1938 her contract offered only $800 per year.

"I would rather walk than board with any school director," Jessie cried to her sisters. "I don't want to be trapped there five days a week. And, besides, I would still have to find a ride at the beginning and the end of each week." Her sister Josephine suggested that Jessie check with the bus service and perhaps the bus might stop at the foot of the hill or at the refractory. Thus, Jessie became a regular on the bus run and on occasion when she missed the bus and started walking, various kind gentlemen on their way to work at the Crescent Division would stop and offer her a ride.

Occasionally, and more often when the workers got to know her and watch for her, some of them would go out of their way to drive Jessie Pifer the remainder of the distance up the hill to her country school. After a time, the men at North American would kid one another about courting "Miss Pifer" (the name she used), most of whom didn't know her marital status. There were several of the workers with whom Jessie became friends, although these friendships went no further than Jessie's being grateful for a ride.

September 19, 1934

Dearest,

I am wondering if you might be writing to me here at the same time.

Monday when I arrived in Cherry Tree I found N.S.[83] in bad shape. Last Friday Dr. Strouth wanted him to go to the hospital and have his foot taken off, but he would not go. He was going on Tuesday morning to Johnstown.

I didn't hear anything from him today as to whether he is still going Sunday. Mother wants me to take her to see him. Last Friday night he tried to end it all. Yes, and none of us knows how to talk with him.

Dear, I am leaving for Baltimore in a few minutes; will write later this week.

All my love,
Doc

Five days later on Monday, September 24 Doc writes again. His mentioning inventory and profit leads one to think he has himself begun to operate the Clover Farm store in Huntingdon to which he referred above.

September 24, 1934

Darling,

Just finished with the inventory and the week's profit. Dear, I sure did miss you over the week-end. It seems so long since we were together.

There is a good dance at Altoona tomorrow. Sure would like to take you, but N. G.'s condition is so bad I expect bad news any minute. Mother and I got to Johnstown about 3 p.m. on Sunday [September 23]. He spoke to me when I went in, but was delirious all the time I was there. They amputated his leg last Thursday above the knee. They didn't expect him to live that night, then they gave him a blood transfusion. It seemed to help [but] his condition was so low on Friday and Saturday they gave up all hope. I really never expect him to come out of the hospital.

Bertha's sister [Bertha is N.G.'s wife] lives just one block from the hospital that makes it convenient. If nothing happens before Saturday I will be over on Saturday night. I will be able to tell you everything then.

I will be waiting for my letter from you.

All my Love,

Doc

The following day Harry writes again from Huntingdon with clear indication of yearning to be with Jessie and he was hopeful that they soon would be together again. His reference to "closing at 6" may also be indicative that he was now working in or operating a grocery store rather than traveling sales. This is supported in a later letter and in the local newspaper in 1951 that Harry Hawes had operated a Clover Farm Store in Huntingdon and then later in Mount Union.

September 25, 1934

Dearest,

Just a note, am going to see [Joan] Crawford and [Clark] Gable in "Chained" tonight.[84] Didn't hear anything from N.J. since we were there Sunday. Probably will tomorrow. I forgot last night to tell you about the big strike in the silk mill[85] here last week. Will tell you about it on Sunday.

This closing at 6 gives me a chance to get caught up in my movies. Last night I worked and tonight I don't have a thing to do. Sure wish you were here. It seems so long these whole weeks; do hope we get settled soon. I wish now you had come over and we were going to the dance tonight but we will soon be together.

All my Love,

Doc

milton
Wed 9 P.M.

Dearest
Darling
Sweety Pie.
Wonder if you are
thinking of me now

arm tonight
nt think
be long
thing will

ll you
I. G. when
ou.
ad was some
far the
e not
tonight last Sun-
iator get
its

you
e not love
the Dae

---

120 ROOMS
EVERY ROOM AN
OUTSIDE EXPOSURE

DIRECTLY ON
THE WM. PENN AND
LAKE TO SEA HIGHWAY

The Coleman Hotel

DINING ROOM
COFFEE SHOPPE

GARAGE
IN CONNECTION

LEWISTOWN, PA., Monday night

Darling
Now in Lewistown
at home. Got things
moved Saturday fixed
up yesterday came
home about 8 last
nig be very tired

mother had
kind of a new
ision yesterday
was first real
go to church
something we
with her my
it became
she Dr don't
to know just
caused it but
better today

SEE THE FAMOUS SEVEN MOUNTAIN DISTRICT—LEWISTOWN NARROWS
THE PICTURESQUE JUNIATA RIVER AND THE BEAUTIFUL BIG VALLEY

STATEMENT

Miss J. Pifer   Aug. 1, 1935

TO DR. G. E HOMAN, DR.
DENTIST
STATE STREET
CURWENSVILLE, PA.

For Professional Services $ 11.50

Miss Pifer, I need some cash bad. I will settle
this for $6.00
Thank You.

In a LITTLE GYPSY TEA ROOM
Lyric by EDGAR LESLIE
Music by JOE BURKE
JOE MORRIS MUSIC Co
-MUSIC PUBLISHERS-
1619 BROADWAY - - - NEW YORK

Letters Letters Letters Letters

1935 1935 1935 1935 1935 1935 1935 1935 1935 1935 1935 1935 1935

At the beginning of 1935 the situation with Harry and Jessie had not changed. She continued to teach in Bridgeport and live in the family home in Curwensville. Harry may have still not been earning enough money to support the two of them. What is clear is that he still was in love with Jessie and hopeful that "things will break" and that he and Jessie soon will be reunited. This letter of February 27 was written from Milton and postmarked in nearby Danville, not far from Williamsport.

February 27, 1935

Dearest Darling, Sweety Pie,

Wonder if you are thinking of me now. How I wish our lips were together at this minute. I have had a good week as far as it has gone thus far.

Rather cold tonight but the radiator sure is doing its good work. So sorry we are not keeping each other warm tonight but I don't think it will be long until things will break and we can be together again.

Will tell you about N.Y. when I see you.

Sure was some snow. The roads were not so good last Sun. but did get through.

Will see you Saturday.

All my Love and Kisses,
Doc

Three weeks later Harry writes from Huntingdon, on stationery from the Coleman Hotel in Lewistown. Since we know that he opened a Clover Farm Grocery Store at some point he may be referring to this when he says they "got things moved Saturday." [86]

March 18, 1935

Darling,

I am not in Lewistown. At home. Got things moved Saturday, fixed up yesterday, came home about 8 last night. Very tired.

Mother had some kind of a nerve condition episode yesterday morning She was ready to go to church when something went wrong with her right arm. It became paralyzed. The Dr. doesn't seem to know just what caused it but it is better today.

He [the doctor] made three trips yesterday, staying about a hour each time. They gave her morphine but it didn't seem to help the pain. For awhile we thought she wasn't going to live. The Doc said today she would be all right in about a week. She must stay in bed and keep very quiet.

I expect to leave for Northumberland in the morning. I will try to be in early on Saturday to see you.

All my Love,

Doc

From all indications Harry fully intended to be reunited with Jessie. Unfortunately, however, the above is the final letter in existence from Harry Hawes to Jessie. While there is no evidence of any kind of falling out, the fact that Terry's birthday card to Jessie in July 1935 is addressed to "Miss Jessie Pifer" suggests that Doc and Jessie either parted ways or that Jessie simply resumed her maiden name.

The birthday card is in the form of a booklet about "Birthday Control" which seems like an odd humor under the circumstances, but perhaps Terry didn't mean it to be any more than a light-hearted birthday greeting.

WHAT IS BIRTHDAY CONTROL?

Most people like to have birthdays but only up to a certain age.

For instance, it is said that the best 10 years of a woman's life is between 29 and 30.

And—
Many a man (especially bachelors) stays 39 until his face gets so old it has whiskers on it.

THAT'S BIRTHDAY CONTROL.

Yes, BIRTHDAY CONTROL has been used since time immaterial.

And why shouldn't 'time' be immaterial as well as one's age, when people these days can have their faces lifted (if they have the 'jack') and can get such swell new paint jobs.

Reconditioning specialists can now arrange it so that a woman can practically 'name her own figure' with new upholstery, anti-knock knees, new stream-lined rumble seats, etc.-etc.

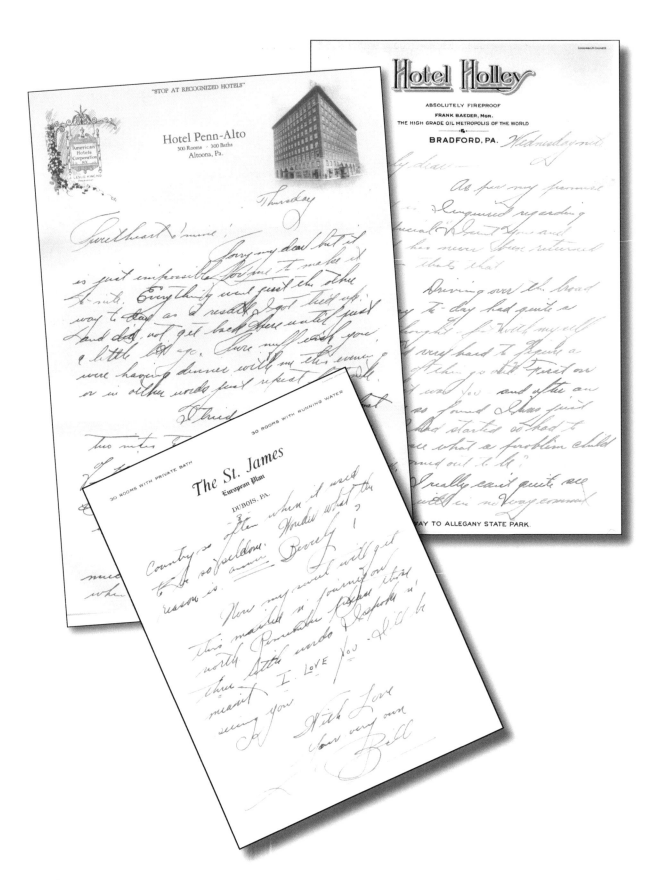

Nineteen-thirty-six was marked by disasters for Curwensville, first with destruction by fire, then by flood. Early in the year, on the bitterly cold Friday night of January 25 with the temperature at zero or below, a kerosene heater exploded in the barbershop of Gilbert Norris. The fire quickly spread through the walls in the adjoining office of the *Curwensville Herald.* From there the flames spread to the Edminston haberdashery and in an easterly direction throughout the next two blocks. The buildings quickly became covered with ice from the water used to fight the fire. At least ten businesses and four homes were lost in the devastation at an estimated total cost of $90,000.[87] The Pifer front porch provided a ringside seat.

Fire was followed by a flood that spring. This March 17 flood, which was precipitated by a quick spring thaw, centered its destruction in the lower Filbert Street area and lowlands bordering Anderson Creek, particularly at its junction with the Susquehanna River. The flood reached the covered bridge at Schofield Street, the Irvin Hill Bridge by the Susquehanna House, and the Filbert Street Bridge, flooding all the surrounding lowlands, and, in effect, separating both Irvin Hill and South Side from the central area of the town.

After such a ruinous winter and spring, by fall the townspeople of Curwensville were ready for something good to happen. And it most definitely did in the form of high school football. The Curwensville Golden Tide became the Western Pennsylvania Football Champions of 1936. Playing for the state championship brought the town together in a frenzy of support for the players and pride in the town itself.

Fall also brought to Jessie Pifer a new gentleman caller named Bill Crawford who first wrote to Jessie from Hotel Holley in Bradford, PA. It is at this point that Jessie began occasionally to introduce herself as "Beverly" in order to first "screen" new men she met. Letters from Bill and some others during this period are addressed to Miss Beverly Pifer.

August 26, 1936

Dear Beverly,

Sure enjoyed yesterday as I have every time I have been with you, my sweet. Cause as I have said before, you are just a little bit of all right and sometime when you know me better (and here is hoping you will), you'll know when I say that it goes pretty deep.

I went on to DuBois and stayed all nite. Am saving the Park Hotel [in Curwensville] until later. Hope the garage is coming OK. [88] Now, my dear, please write me at once if you will, care of "the Fort Pitt Hotel, Pittsburgh" so I can pick it up Monday on my way to Ohio. Perchance I may be back to you next week if my plans work out, but please send the letter.

Best regards to your mother. Now how should I read your "maybe?"

Yours, Bill

Two and a half weeks later (September 11, 1936) Bill writes from the Hotel Penn-Alto in Altoona.

September 11, 1936

Sweetheart mine,

Sorry my dear but it is just impossible for me to make it tonight. Everything went just the other way today and, as a result, I got tied up and did not get back here until just a little bit ago. Sure 'nuff' wish you were having dinner with me this evening or, in other words, I would like to just repeat last night.

I tried very hard the last two nights to give you a small idea of just how I felt toward you and just how much you mean, Sweet. Please believe me when I say that it is pretty awful much.

O, well, I'm just not much good at writing or talking when you are the subject because as I told you before so often, I like you too much!

Now, my dear, I'm going to try very hard to get back Tuesday. Don't be forgetting me until then. You need not answer this note as I cannot tell you where I will be, but in return for letting you off so easy I will expect you to have plenty to say Tuesday. Until then,

Love, Bill

Four days later Bill, totally enthralled, writes so that Jessie receives another letter from him on Thursday before he sees her again. This time he is in DuBois, at the St. James. He, like most of Jessie's suitors, also questions that he has to write to her twice before she writes back once. He pleads that he is not very good at writing letters.

September 15, 1936

Sweetheart of mine:

It sure is not so long ago since I left you, but as I was thinking coming to writing this, it might be best to stop here and drop you a letter so you will be sure to get it on Thursday cause see I want a letter back..

Listen to another secret, sweet. It was most mighty hard to leave you this evening and you don't know just how near I was to turning back, but this account in Bradford just must be taken care of.

Speaking of this "n" that, remember the little poem I started to quote this p.m. Well, it ends, "The brown eyes lower fell because you see I love you," and that was the remark I had hoped to get you to make. However, I guess you did not set me down when you said that was something you would not say until you really were sure you meant it. So--- maybe--- that time will come. I'm hoping so at least, and you can bet your life I'll do my best to make it come very, very soon.

You see, darling, you rather put me on a spot when I have to write two letters before getting one cause see I've tried to tell you my dear that I'm not much good at it and I've not had much practice for such a long, long time.

I'll be looking for you in Altoona on Tuesday! Seems funny to me how I can arrange to be in this section of the country so often when it used to be so seldom. You know what the reason is: Beverly.

Now, my sweet, I will get this mailed and journey on north. Remember please those three little words I spoke and meant, I LOVE YOU. I'll be seeing you.

With Love,

Your Very Own, Bill

Two days pass and Bill may be exhausted at the thought of writing a letter without having one of Jessie's to which to reply. Thus, from Meadville, on September 17, 1935, he sends only a preprinted card with the following message:

Bill is then never heard from again.

Faithful Terry sends a Christmas card from Chicago. There is no personal message, just a card from a friend—a friend who had promised to always be there for Jessie. We can't help but wonder whether Terry has simply decided not to be vulnerable any longer.

JOLLY WISHES

May this be the happiest, merriest, jolliest Christmas you ever had in all your life !

Union Hotel
Blairsville Pa.
July 6 - 38

Hello Darlin
Here I am just as I promised
a letter to you. but how I which I
could deliver it in person
I arrived yesterday A.M. after seven
hrs. train rideing and what a place
to come to. State College was bad
enough but this place has it stopped
I was never so disgusted with every
thing in general. The Town, the job,
and myself. I had planned to
stop over in Curwinsville for two
days on my way up here from Phila.
but had to come by train at the last
moment. And what a hovel this Hotel
is they ask, and get $18.00 a wk. board
and room two in a room. no closet
to hang your clothes in. its either
a rack or the door knob Ye Gods and
small fishes when I look at it I
feel like going off the Water Wagon
and break a three years record I was
trying for in Sept.
all I need is for someone to offer me a
highball right now and I'll be a
first class Toper again. But it seems

Union House
Blairsville, Pa.
July 1, 1938

Hello! Sweets—
Forgive me "Darlin" for not keep
ing my promise in not writing to
you last nite. But Sleep caught
up with me again and I'm makeing sure
I'm writing this before supper. and
it's hot here I believe Sweets you took
the cool breezes away with you when you
left. How did you get home were you
tired? I didn't envy you your journey
But I sure did appreciate your
coming over and your kindness to
me while you were here It shall
remain in the tenderest of my memories
thanks Darlin a million times
Well heres some local scandal
Roy and Slant eyes are not that
way about each other anymore
it seems they had a battle Roy
te about where they should go
and Roy won, that is he thought
he did. They went out to mount
ain View Hotel for dinner, that is
Roy, Nancy, Joe, Geo. and Dan.

Hello Darlin
Your sweet letters arrived
in due time and indeed
it was a pleasant surprise
to hear from you again
I've had quite a exciting week
here (no Darlin not what your
thinking)
It seems these quick
steamfitters are
out of work.
they deci
in on
ruling
memb
have to
to ggl
in
to be
has gone (S
needless to say
as if you didn't know what
I was thrilled about!
But alas and alak it was

I still remain under your
Spell. next week
Love
Vincent

1938 brought with it the House Un-American Activities Committee, the Lambeth Walk[89] and the Benny Goodman band, foreshadowing the "big band" sound, soon to be a major influence on American music. For the general worker in business and industry, the important matter of the year was that the 40-hour week became the standard. Offices began to close on Saturday mornings, providing the foundation for the concept of "free" week-ends. Retail stores that remained open on Saturdays began arranging rotating schedules so that their employees also could work a 40-hour week.

One indication of a slight upward trend in the economy was that by the late 1930s nail polish, first advertised in 1936, was gaining popularity with those who could afford it and who had the chutzpah to wear it. Jessie longed to be among those with bright red nails, but still could not afford any extravagance and could not yet think of any rationale to convince herself—let alone her father— otherwise. Even though she was thirty years old and had been married, she still tried to be considerate of her father's opinion on such matters since she lived under his roof.

Another sign that nationally things were beginning to return to normal and that society was again gaining attention was the advent of traveling public speakers who provided lectures on the etiquette of cigarette smoking. One such presentation was given to the members of the Society of New York State Women, addressing the habits and manners that make smoking objectionable, demonstrating ways to avoid the objections and to use smoking as a means to reflect social graces.[90]

The event for which 1938 is most remembered, however, occurred on Halloween Eve with the radio broadcast of a fictional radio drama, Orson Welles' "War of the Worlds." The program was so convincing that, despite announcements to the contrary, many listeners believed that the world actually was being invaded by Martians. As a result, a short-lived but intense panic gripped the country.

The late 1930s were strange and uncertain times. Young people were worried about the future, yet because of the lack of international news, much was simply speculation. One thing, however, was consistent. Those unattached could find opportunities to meet others similarly situated at the dancing clubs and public venues that were popping up or being converted from something else (some from amusement parks) all over the country. Most important these dance halls were within driving distance of most small towns and those in their twenties and thirties flocked to these "ballrooms."

Jessie continued in her love of dancing and she enjoyed the socializing promoted by clubs, either local or some distance from Curwensville, which she preferred as it had always been difficult for a teacher to participate in activities others could take for granted. The Sunset Ballroom in Ebensburg, a large structure built just for dancing, was the closest to a nightclub atmosphere most people in central Pennsylvania ever had experienced and was one of the many halls that were becoming even more popular as America came out of the Depression. Sunset booked most of what would become the "Big Bands" and had no trouble filling their hall, built in the woods outside of town.

Such ballrooms were a mecca for the plethora of traveling salesmen, most of them young and many of them unmarried. Unlike the "taxi-dancehalls" in the larger cities, these small town venues did not provide "girls for hire"—usually at ten cents a dance—as dancing partners. Rather, young singles— or foursomes of two married couples traveling together—flocked to these halls.

It is likely that Jessie met Vincent Hughes either at Sunset Ballroom or at the Oriental Ballroom in Gallitzin, both of which were close to Blairsville. Jessie always knew the latest dance steps, was attractive and personable, and enjoyed meeting new people. She never lacked for a dance partner.

After meeting Jessie, Vincent Hughes writes from the Union Hotel in Blairsville, using the name Jessie (rather than the recently used "Beverly") Pifer in the address, so Vincent must have passed muster with Jessie.

July 6, 1938

Hello Darlin,

Here I am, just as I promised a letter to you, but how I wish I could deliver it in person. I arrived yesterday a.m. after several hours train riding and what a place to come to. State College was bad enough but this place has it stopped. I was never so disgusted with everything in general, the town, the job, and myself.

I had planned to stop over in Curwensville for two days on my way up here from Philadelphia, but had to come by train at the last moment. And what a hovel this Hotel is. They ask, and get, $18.00 a week board and room two in a room. No closet to hang your clothes in—it's either a rack or the door knob. Ye Gods and small fishes, when I look at it I feel like going off the water wagon and break a three-year record I was trying for by September.

All I need is for someone to offer me a highball right now and I'll be a first class you-know-what again. But it seems the more time I spend composing this tale of woe to you, Sweets, I feel better, so I hope I finish before I get the offer of the highball. Drunk is one condition I'd never want you to see me in.

Did John come over Saturday and what kind of a friend did he bring along? I've been worried about that right along, afraid he might bring along some good looking bright young student from Pitt; and that would be the end of "poor me" with you.

But I think you'll keep your promise and think of me once in awhile and if you do I'll be satisfied with my lot, even Blairsville, because, Darlin, I think you're the grandest and most understanding person I've ever met. At least the memory of you has continued to linger with me longer than anyone I can remember and that, Sweets, coming from me, when you get to know me better, you'll say is something. I could explain that last statement better in person than I can write it. I know you will understand.

Devotedly, Vincent

Five days later Vincent again writes from the Union Hotel in Blairsville

July 11, 1938

Hello, Sweets —

Forgive me "Darlin" for not keeping my promise of writing to you last nite. But sleep caught up with me again. So I'm making sure I'm writing this before supper and is it hot here! I believe, Sweets, you took the cool breezes away with you when you left. How did you get home, were you tired? I didn't envy you your journey.

But I sure did appreciate your coming over and your kindness to me while you were here. It shall live in the tenderest of my memories. Thanks, Darlin, a million times.

When am I going to see you again? I hope it's before you are stopped again from "going swimming?"!!X?!!??? But in any event it will be good to see you again no matter where it is.

And with that, My Pet, I'll come to a close hoping this finds you well, cool and happy.

As Ever, Vincent

Not unexpectedly, Vincent is waiting for a return letter from Jessie. He waits her out for a month and then sends her a card from Blairsville.

Also enclosed is a longer written message in which Vincent pokes fun at himself and softens the message in the card.

September 11, 1938

Hello Darlin,

What's the trouble? Have you crossed me off your mailing list?

I was almost afraid of that! and I don't scare easily either.

Be that as it may, one could hardly blame you. You've seen me at my best, and at my worst. (But if you've seen Wallace Beery in the "Good Old Soak" then you've met yours truly at my absolute worse.)

And neither one I'm sure has left any pleasant thoughts of me in your mind. How could they? But on the other hand, you've left an impression on me that will stay with me for a long, long time. An impression that one associates with everything that is lovely and Jessie, dear, I shall always think of you as just that, no matter where I may go.

As Ever,, Vincent

Jessie must have cared enough about Vincent to write to him and he responds, again from Blairsville, with great eagerness to see her again, hopefully the coming week-end.

September 26, 1938

Hello Darlin,

Your sweet letter arrived in due time and indeed it was a pleasant surprise to hear from you again. I had quite an exciting week here (No, Darlin, not what you're thinking.) It seems there's quite a few steam fitters and helpers out of work in Pittsburgh, so they decided to squeeze those still on this job by a fake ruling that those not regular members from Pittsburgh would have to go. Well, I was all set to go back to State College; in fact I was all packed to go and this strike happened, dammit.

You can imagine how I felt about this. But it was called off at the last moment. I am the only one allowed to stay. Now, I ask you, Dearest, don't take the icing off the cake so it looks like I'm good for a long stay here.

You mentioned in your letter that you had your doubts about what spell or influence I was under when I wrote you last. Darlin, if you meant corn squeezings, you're wrong. I haven't had a drink since you left. But the spell, well, you can take the blame for that. I wrote that letter with the thought that I had been forgotten by the Girl I couldn't forget. I sure was down in the dumps that week-end everyone had gone home. I'd have given anything to have been able to talk to you, but I had no way to get in touch with you.

I had company from State last Sunday night. John's sister stopped on her way back from Pitt. They brought John to school – when I say "they" I mean Charlotte and her boyfriend. So have no fears. I was not alone with her. In fact, I've not been alone with anyone since you were here (do I hear you laughing?). That's the truth, Sweet. I've been so good I'm ready to spread wings. How about next week-end? Can you come over? I'd love to see you again.

I'm going to Pittsburgh Saturday morning to buy some clothes and will be back early in the evening. So Darlin, how about calling me Thursday or Friday evening about eight o'clock and let me know if you can make it and Darlin, please don't say no.

Hoping this finds you well and happy and to see you next week-end. I still remain under your spell.

Love, Vincent

It seems fitting that this collection of letters closes near the end of the 1930s with a Western Union Telegram, at that time the means by which to reach someone quickly, and far different from the handwritten letters which reveal the care the writers took to craft them. We can envision these suitors—with or without their photos—by their choice of words, their grammar, their style of phrasing, and their sincerity. And, above all, we are touched by the devotion to and love for Jebbie expressed by all these gentlemen callers.

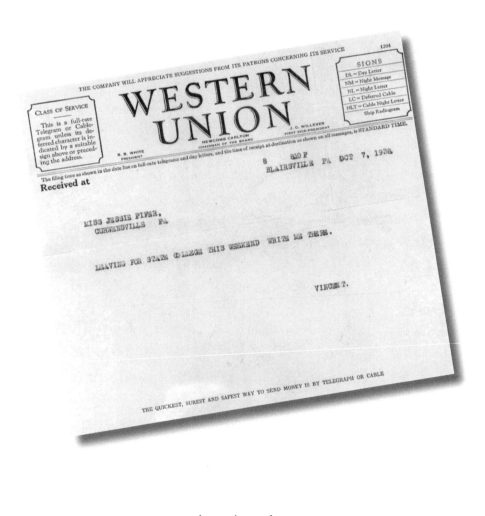

Late 1930s

As the clouds of conflict gathered on the world's horizon, Jessie was only one of most Americans who were very uncertain of what the future might hold. Hitler had been collecting European countries from the time he had met with his foreign minister and his top generals on November 5, 1937 and had announced his plans for acquiring new territory for Germany in Europe's heartland. In only one year's time Hitler had brought under his rule Austria and the Sudeten Germans. Then in 1939, breaking solemn promises he had made to heads of state in Europe, he moved his army into Prague, dividing the remainder of Czechoslovakia into two German satellite states.

At the same time, the Japanese militarists were beginning their aggression in an aim to build an empire in East Asia. As part of their plans they made a concerted effort to drive American and European missionary, educational, medical, and cultural activities out of China. American churches, hospitals, schools, and colleges were bombed in Chinese cities despite flag markings on their roofs—to this time always honored, and many American missionaries and their families were killed. There were so many "accidents" of this sort that a cynic reported the most dangerous spot to be in an air raid was in an American mission.

In 1939 the Japanese captured Shanghai and proceeded to make life intolerable for Americans and Europeans in the international settlement. Then, suddenly and without warning, on September 1, 1939 Germany attacked Poland. Two days later Britain and France declared war on Germany and the British dominions followed suit shortly, in effect beginning World War II and changing life forever—in Curwensville and in the larger world.

Epilogue

ecause I came to know these gentlemen callers through their letters to Jebbie, I felt close to them and wanted to know what had become of them after their letters ceased. I met with less than moderate success in locating them, but I have documented here the information I could trace and verify. It is fitting to not let these gentlemen go unheralded.

Almost twenty years ago when I was beginning the research that became the story of *Jebbie: Vamp to Victim* (the companion biography to this book), online resources were slim or non-existent, so I had only the documents from my Aunt Jessie's effects to use as pieces to the puzzle. Because Jessie had not returned William L. Fowler's high school yearbook, The *1925 Clarionette,* I thought I would be able to find some answers about him there.

To my dismay I discovered that none of the photographs in the yearbook were identified, so I wasn't sure at first which male senior was Bill and who might be John Ditz, Bill's best friend, and both suitors of Jessie Pifer. Because I knew that Bill Fowler was on the school basketball team and that John Ditz served as manager, I was able to make an educated guess by matching the brief descriptions under their senior photos with the photo of the basketball team.

And so the search was on!

With only this information I wrote to the superintendent at Clarion Area School District to ask if the names Fowler or Ditz were familiar to anyone at the school or if he could tell me if any family members of either Fowler or Ditz might still be in the area. At the time I was more interested in finding Fowler because I believed the yearbook should be returned to the family. The superintendent replied that he was not from the area but would make inquiries and he would let me know. (This was pre-email days for many of us and I heard nothing further from him.)

Ten years later as the biography of Jessie began to take shape and I realized that both Bill and John had corresponded with her, I began to try to find more information about them, but with very limited success. Many times I tried a search on the Internet, but with no results. About seven years ago I subscribed to "Newspaper Archives," an online service, and began what I thought would be a systematic search. However, many of the small town newspapers were not yet in the archives of the newspaper site, so that search was not fruitful. At that time I had only a few greeting cards and a handful of letters that I had found in Jessie's desk. These letters, in addition to comments Jessie had written in her scrapbook, continued to be all I had to make connections to and assumptions about these two gentlemen who appeared to be close friends.

John I. Ditz

Discovering the cache of letters in Aunt Jessie's steamer trunk and noting the number of letters **John I. Ditz** had written to her led me to a fresh search for him. Also, because the content of these letters suggested that John Ditz may have returned to Clarion to live, he became the focus of my research and I began my pursuit anew.

Parker D. Cramer

Since Ditz had written letters to Jessie using letterhead from the Cramer-Bartow Airport I searched this name and found an email address from an airport site that included the name Cramer. My excitement increased when I had a response from a man who held the surname of Cramer. He said he was not related to the Cramer who had owned the Cramer-Bartow Airport, nor was he related to Parker Cramer, the well-known aviator who had lived in Clarion.

The flying field, which was the first municipally-owned airport in the United States, was home to pioneer pilot Parker D. Cramer, only the fourth person in the United States to be issued a pilot's license. The airport was named in Cramer's honor after he and his crew were lost on a route-mapping flight over the North Sea in 1931. A year later papers belonging to Parker Cramer were found floating in the sea off the Shetland Islands. These included a letter to his mother, his pilot's license, and a description of the plane in which he was making his fatal, final flight.

I later discovered that John Ditz had been interested in flying and in the fall of 1926, according to *The Oil City Derrick* (Oil City, September 4, 1926, page 1) Ditz, a student at the University of Pennsylvania, was a passenger in a small private airplane which crashed shortly after take-off when attempting to climb too fast in a strong wind which caught the plane, then threw it into a spin. The quick-thinking pilot, Dean Lamb, was able to guide the plane from a spin into a slide as it crashed to earth from 200 feet in the air. Ditz was said to have been jarred and bruised in addition to losing several teeth.

During still another attempt to locate information on John I. Ditz I found a website for the Clarion County Historical Society whose museum is named and housed in "The Sutton-Ditz House." I immediately began the first of a series of email inquiries. Following a response from the Museum Director—and an offer from a classmate who lived in Shippenville (only two miles from Clarion) to introduce me to a friend of hers who had lived in Clarion most of her life, in October 2011 I made what I hoped would be a journey of discovery.

The Sutton-Ditz House

A four-hour drive led me to not only the museum, but also to the whole town. On Main Street I saw first hand the original location of the A.G. Corbett Drugstore, where Jessie had first met Bill Fowler and John Ditz, and the hardware store, then known as the Ditz and Mooney Hardware Store that had been established by John Ditz's father (whose name was John A. Ditz). We then found the original site (near Clarion Normal School) of the high school attended by best friends Fowler and Ditz. Next we sought out the addresses of several (former) rooming houses where Jessie had lived during summer sessions (however, it is likely that some of the streets had been renumbered as they were in Curwensville, so that, in some cases, the house numbers of the 1920s may not be the same properties with these numbers today). We ended the tour—and our quest—with John Ditz's family home (now the museum) on 5th Avenue and John's own home as a married adult, not far from the hardware store on Main Street.

I learned that in 1908 John A. Ditz and his wife had acquired their property (which would become the childhood home of their son, John I.) opposite the Public Square that contained Thomas Sutton's 1844 law office, the 1847 Sutton house, and several small buildings along the lot's Fifth Avenue frontage. Early the following year, the senior Ditz began a major remodeling of the house, a project which converted the formerly Greek Revival style residence into an imposing Neo-Classical Revival style home, complete with a dominating centered portico on the facade.

As noted in the narrative accompanying the letters in this collection, in the 1920s the senior Mr. Ditz suffered financial losses as a result of investing in a "Florida land scheme" and the Ditz family was reduced to modifying their spacious home to the purpose of a Tourist Home. Following the death of Mr. Ditz, his wife continued to rent "every available space" in the house, according to the present museum director.

Somewhat surprisingly, the Sutton-Ditz Museum House contains only three items belonging to the Ditz family—among them a piano and a case for tickets used for admission to the Frampton Opera House, which, like opera houses in many small towns, was part of a larger building, in this case one occupied by the Ditz and Mooney Hardware Company. This hardware store was considered to be the leading purveyor of hardware, buggies, wagons, and farm implements and was one of the largest such retailers in the area.

White Pillars

The house of John A.'s son, John I. Ditz, was originally built for banker Walter Graham. Known as the White Pillars because of its architectural double porticoes supported by fluted columns with Ionic capitals, the style of the house is reminiscent of the Ditz family home. Originally serving only as the residence of Mr. and Mrs. Ditz, part of the White Pillars later became the Ditz White Pillar Gift Shop after the original gift shop outgrew its space in one end of the hardware store that John I. had purchased from his father. And, yes, John did complete his education at the University of Pennsylvania, from which many letters had been sent to Jessie.

It was only a short drive to the original Cramer-Bartow Airport, now the Cramer Marina used to store watercraft, but is still the same building shown in earlier photographs of the hangar. There I met William E. Culbertson, the owner. He kindly listened to my inquiries, telling me that he and his mother had both known John I. Ditz. Mr. Culbertson then telephoned his mother to ask if she would speak with us. Mrs. Culberson was most charming and helpful to me, a complete stranger, and I wish I had had more time with her. Her husband and John I. Ditz had been good friends, sharing an interest in aviation and stock car racing. Mrs. Culbertson also had known Parker Cramer. In fact, she shared with me newspaper clippings regarding the airport and the exploits of Parker Cramer.

The last bit of information I have on John I. Ditz is from his obituary, recording that he had died on April 2, 1980. The article also revealed that Ditz had been an only child and had no children of his own and no direct descendants.

Terry McGovern

I also was very curious about **F. X. ("Terry") McGovern** who had been devoted to Jessie and wrote to her faithfully for a longer length of time than any other suitor among the gentlemen callers. I was completely captivated by his devotion. Terry was graduated from Coalport High School, possibly in 1922; however, this high school no longer exists either in name or in structure. It is also unlikely that Terry returned to his home town of Coalport or to Clymer where his family had moved when he was in his twenties. In addition, the name "Terry (or even F.X., probably Francis Xavier) McGovern" turned out to be a fairly common name in the United States. Further, I could not narrow his location since Terry worked for AT&T based in Chicago, from which he was relocated several times, including to cities in Wisconsin and Minnesota.

Harry "Doc" Hawes

My interest in **Harry Benjamin "Doc" Hawes** also went deep because in March of 1930 Jessie married Doc Hawes. They had eloped, and my mother spoke his name only in a hushed tone— even at that only once or twice. This was, of course, a time when children did not ask questions, particularly of such matters, and was not something I would have asked details about at any time.

Harry (Doc) Hawes on the right

While my mother never spoke ill of Doc Hawes, I had a mental picture of him as a dark character in Aunt Jessie's life. It was after *Jebbie: Vamp to Victim* had been written and was in the hands of the publisher that I discovered the cache of love letters. While these letters certainly did not paint Doc as a villain, they did present a puzzle in that after a year of marriage Jessie returned to her family home to live. This situation remained for several years during which time Doc wrote to her, mentioning that he missed her and referencing that he would see her "on the week-end." Then his letters suddenly ended in 1935—or perhaps Jessie just didn't keep them beyond that time, although she had many letters from other gentlemen after this date.

I was able to verify that Hawes had been born in Cherry Tree on October 24, 1899 to Boyd W. (listed as a blacksmith in several places, then as a merchant [possibly a grocer, based on references Harry made in his letters]) and Rosa Patrick Hawes. At the time of Harry Hawes' death in 1951 he was survived by a brother, John, who lived in Atlanta, Georgia, and two sisters, Mary, of Tyrone, and Mrs. C. H. Anderson of Cleveland, Ohio.

Recently I did find an archival news story about Harry Hawes on the front page of *The Daily News* (November 20, 1951, Huntingdon and Mount Union) which recounted that Mr. Hawes had died unexpectedly of a heart attack. He was a popular grocer at the time, had owned a grocery store (possibly a Clover Farm store which may have been named Hawes Market) at the corner of Sixteenth and Mifflin Streets in Huntingdon, and at the time of his death was operating Hawes Market in Mount Union. The article also mentioned he had been married in 1949 to Bernadine Wert. No surviving children were mentioned so presumably he was childless.

In October 2011 I visited Huntingdon and found the building that had housed his grocery store at the corner of Sixteenth and Mifflin Streets. The building has a side entrance as well and may be where the photo (that appears above) of Harry Hawes and "Shorty" Henderson was taken.

Other Gentlemen Callers

I was completely unsuccessful in finding anyone in Clarion who recalled **William L. Fowler** or a family by the name of Fowler. I had hoped that Bill Fowler, having been class president and an athlete in high school, would have been remembered by someone I could identify, but such was not the case. His family likely were persons of means because Bill Fowler, like his best friend John Ditz, attended the University of Pennsylvania.

I also could find nothing on Fowler in "Newspaper Archives," but Clarion newspapers are not part of this database. I tried several other searches (including the date of this writing in December 2011) but have had not success. If anyone who reads this book can help me locate further information on William L. Fowler, Class of 1925, Clarion High School, who then attended University of Pennsylvania, or leads on any other correspondents introduced herein, please let me know.

I can be reached at jtwitmer@aol.com or yesteryearpublishing@gmail.com.

Endnotes

1   Letter to Jessie from Terry McGovern, July 31, 1928.

2   Coontz, p. 194.

3   Bailey, p. 13.

4   The practice of "petting" was exclusively an American institution.

5   Frith, p. 235.

6   Terkel, in referring to his book *Hard Times*.

7   Schrum, p. 113.

8   Modell, p. 72.

9   Rothman, p. 190.

10   Frith, p. 187, quoting Paula Fass's book.

11   Modell, p. 74.

12   Witmer, pp. 83-84.

13   Riegel & Long, p. 267.

14   Morison, p. 908.

15   The word "necking" seems to have originated in the 1920s, as noted in *The Girl Graduate* and in a personal letter from Terry McGovern to Jessie Pifer, July 21, 1928.

16   *Oil*, Upton Sinclair, p. 202.

17   Paula S. Fass, p. 153.

18   *The Girl Graduate,* designed and illustrated by Louise Perrett and Sarah K. Smith, The Reilly and Lee Co., Chicago.

19   Class History, *The Echo,* 1924, p. 72.

20   Class History, *The Echo,* 1924, p. 72.

21   Class History, *The Echo,* 1924, p. 72.

22   Graduation announcement, Curwensville High School, Class of 1924.

23   *The Girl Graduate.*

24   "Wings" was the first film, and the only silent film ever, to win the Academy Award for Best Picture.

25   This 1927 silent film was directed by the celebrated director Josef von Sternberg.

26   A 1928 silent film starring Mary Astor.

27   A 1928 silent film starring Charlie Chaplin.

28   An earlier silent film directed by Jean Hersholt.

29   Fred Waring started with a troupe known as Waring's Banjazztra in early '20s. As the '20s progressed, the troupe became known as Waring's Pennsylvanians.

30   The Pennsylvania State College *Woman's Handbook,* 1924. Section reprinted in *The Penn Stater,* July/August 2001, p. 45.

31   Personal collection of the author.

32   Teacher's Contract, September 4, 1924.

33   Walter Shreffler, Class of '26, Clarion, on the basketball team with, and a friend of, Bill Fowler. Jessie likely had a date with him and told Terry she couldn't come to Coalport to see him (Terry) because of this.

Endnotes

34 Terry is referring here to Winfield Sykes whom Jessie also dated.

35 An early silent film star.

36 Mary Garden was a well-known operatic soprano who also starred in two silent films made by Samuel Goldwyn in 1917 and 1928.

37 Interestingly, the term "blind date" was first used in the 1920s, originated by college students; and, according to *Dictionary of American Slang,* 3rd edition, the word "date" was not widely used until 1925.

38 John I. Ditz's father's name was John A. Ditz. The family was well-known and the town was small, so using only Clarion without the street address of 17 S. 5th Avenue would be sufficient.

39 Walter "Red" Shreffler.

40 Likely the afternoon sulky races at Indiana or Cambria County Fair as the Clearfield County Fair was held earlier (five weeks before Labor Day).

41 What John Ditz's letter does not reveal is the information that his parents were at this time suffering a significant financial loss in the unsuccessful Florida land speculation of 1925. Mr. Ditz was part owner of the very successful Ditz and Mooney Hardware Company, the leading purveyor of hardware, buggies, wagons, and farm implements in the area. In 1909 he had begun a major remodeling of a large (later historic and on the National Register) Revival style home. The property is now the home of the Historical Society and is known as the Sutton-Ditz House.

42 *Coed* is also an informal term for a female student attending a formerly all-male college or university (or any university). This usage reflects the historical process by which it was often female pupils who were admitted to schools originally reserved for boys, and thus it was they who were identified with its becoming "coeducational."

43 Very possibly this young man is of the family who had established the (Bill) Cramer and (Red) Bartow airfield, later named the Parker Cramer Airport, since there is evidence of John Ditz having a friend there.

44 The BBG CO was the Berney-Bond Glass Company (1905-1930) located in Clarion and other places. Most of these plants were closed down in later years, until by the early 1970s only the Clarion plant was still making bottles.

45 Presumably he had sent an earlier telegram and, in typical fashion, Jessie would have ignored it.

46 Evans, p. 182.

47 A classmate from Clarion. No other information found on his name. Only the nickname appears in any of the mention of him by others and by his writing in Jessie's *Girl Graduate* memory book.

48 Jessie's mother's sister, Rosanna (Rosie) Stormer, lived in DuBois. Jessie learned at an early age that relatives can be useful.

49 Chautauqua was a popular education movement for adults in the late 19th and early 20th centuries, bringing entertainment and cultural programs to communities with speakers, musicians, and other specialists of the day.

50 The Auburn was a highly prized, luxury vehicle, part of a partnership that offered Auburns, Cords and Duesenbergs. In high school John had a Chalmers, an expensive car for the time.

51 RPO is for Railroad Post Office and was a special mail car on a train for letters mailed from train stations and sent by passengers.

52 Allen, *Only Yesterday*, p. 76.

53 Sinclair, *Oil.*

54 April 8, 1928. He was getting his bid in early.

Endnotes

55   Jessie's sister Kate and Tommy's brother Howard married in June that year and some years later became the parents of Judith Thompson Witmer who prepared this publication and is the niece of Jessie Pifer.

56   Allen, *The Big Change*, p. 123.

57   Allen, *The Big Change*, p. 124.

58   John would be traveling by train; hence the direct route to Pittsburgh, then a local to Clarion.

59   This is further indication of the financial difficulties mentioned in endnote #41. By 1930 the Ditz property had been converted into tourists rooms, likely as a result of Mr. Ditz's losses, although the family continued to live in the home.

60   The Hupmobile was a popular medium-priced car. The company was known for its many innovations, but when it moved into the higher priced bracket, it lost its established clientele and never regained its hold on the market.

61   Wilbur Daniel Steele, Grosset & Dunlap, 1927.

62   This likely is further indication of the financial difficulties faced by John's father.

63   Terry was Catholic; Jessie was Presbyterian, a real concern at this time in history.

64   The tour consisted of taking off from New York July 20 and sailing to Europe to tour Amsterdam, Venice, Rome, Paris, London and other stops and returning September 2.

65   The Fisher Building, which contains the 2,089-seat Fisher Theatre, is an ornate Art Deco Skyscraper built in 1928 and constructed of limestone, granite, and marble. It was financed by the Fisher family with proceeds from the sale of Fisher Body to General Motors.

66   Likely these are the popular flat caps that later were known as newsboy caps.

67   Bezilla, p. 136.

68   Allen, *Only Yesterday*, p. 81.

69   Indicating it had been mailed at a railroad terminal.

70   *DuBois Courier*, July 9, 1929 noted, "Rev. Edgar Neff, of the Episcopal Church of the Advent, Birmingham, Alabama, spent the week-end visiting with Neal Buchanan at his home on Knarr Street."

71   Now the Alcott Hotel, Cape May's second-oldest operating hotel, debuted in 1878.

72   Dubbed "The Orchid Lady of the Screen," Griffith was one of the most popular film actresses of the 1920s and widely considered the most beautiful actress of the silent screen.

73   A classical revival architectural-styled hotel, its significant years are listed as 1925-1949. Now on the National Register of Historical Buildings. At the time it was one of a chain of Schroeder Hotels, one of which in Milwaukee advertised 850 rooms, 850 baths, a major upgrade to typical offerings.

74   Hagerstown, Maryland was the popular place to which Central Pennsylvanians went to elope.

75   Today this would be called a compact (or vanity compact) or a make-up kit.

76   It is interesting to note that the term "girl friend" did not originate with the modern Valley Girls.

77   While the term Victrola applies ONLY to internal horn phonographs made by the Victor Talking Machine Company, and is *not* a generic term for all old phonographs, the shortened form became the slang term for any phonograph. They were very expensive, a basic one selling for $100 ($1900 in today's money).

78   Evans, p. 228.

79   Allen, *Since Yesterday*, p. 110.

Endnotes

80   Allen, *Since Yesterday*, p. 110.

81   Allen, *Since Yesterday*, p. 110.

82   Allen, *Since Yesterday*, p. 111.

83   Research has identified him as Harry's uncle, N. G. Hawes, who died in July 1935 from, according to the *Huntingdon Daily News*, complications "of a condition he had been battling."

84   *Huntingdon Daily News*, September 24, 1934.

85   Susquehanna Silk Mills in Huntingdon and other locations. Mills were cutting wages in many parts of the country.

86   Research has revealed that Harry "Doc" Hawes was, indeed, a grocery salesman, then later operated a grocery store in Huntingdon (His own father was a grocer in Cherry Tree), and then in Mount Union.

87   Morgan, p. 126.

88   Jessie's father was rebuilding a shed into a garage for his well drilling equipment.

89   The Lambeth Walk was a popular walking dance, done in a jaunty strutting style, copied from the musical "Me and My Girl." It became almost a craze in the better night clubs.

90   "Clubwomen Get Lessons in Cigaret Smoking," *Life 50 Years*, Special Anniversary Issue, Fall 1986, p. 87.

References
(In addition to the letters)

Allen, Frederick Lewis. *The Big Change*. NY: Bantam Books, 1952.

Allen, Frederick Lewis. *Only Yesterday*. NY: John Wiley, reprinted 1997.

Allen, Frederick Lewis. *Since Yesterday*. NY: Bantam Books, 1961.

Bailey, Beth L. *From Front Porch to Back Seat: Courtship in Twentieth-Century America*. Baltimore: Johns Hopkins University Press, 1988.

Bezilla, Michael. *Penn State, An Illustrated History*. University Park, PA: Penn State University Press, 1985.

"Clubwomen Get Lessons in Cigaret Smoking," *Life 50 Years*, Special Anniversary Issue. Fall 1986.

Coontz, Stephanie. *The Way We Never Were*. NY: Basic Books, 1992.

Evans, Harold. *The American Century*. NY: Alfred A. Knopf, 1998.

Fass, Paula S. *The Damned and the Beautiful*. NY: Oxford University Press, 1977.

Frith, Simon. *Sound Effects: Youth, Leisure, and the Politics of Rock 'n' Roll*. NY: Pantheon Books, 1981.

Huntingdon Daily News, Huntingdon, PA. September 24, 1934.

Modell, John. *Into One's Own: From Youth to Adulthood in the United States, 1920-1975*. Los Angeles: University of California Press, 1989.

Morgan, Edward, ed., *Curwensville in Celebration of 200 Years*, Bicentennial Committee, May 1999.

Morison, Samuel Eliot. *The Oxford History of the American People*. NY: Oxford University Press, 1965.

Oil City Derrick, Oil City, September 4, 1926, p. 1.

Perrett, Louise and Sarah K. Smith, Designers and Illustrators. *The Girl Graduate*. Chicago, IL: The Reilly and Lee Co., n. d.

Riegel, Robert E. and David F. Long. *The American Story, Volume Two:* Maturity. NY: McGraw-Hill, 1955.

Rothman, Ellen K. *Hands and Hearts:* A History of Courtship in America. NY: Basic Books, Inc., 1984.

Schrum, Kelly. *Some Wore Bobby Sox: The Emergence of Teenage Girls' Culture, 1920-1945*. New York: Palgrave Macmillan, 2004.

Sinclair, Upton. *Oil*. NY: Penguin, 2007, originally published 1927.

Steele, Wilbur Daniel. *Meat*. NY: Grosset & Dunlap, 1928.

Terkel, Studs. *Hard Times*. NY: Pantheon, 1970.

The 1924 Echo, Curwensville High School, Curwensville, PA.

The 1925 Clarionette, Clarion High School Clarion, PA.

The Daily News, Huntingdon and Mount Union, PA, November 20, 1951, p. 1.

The Derrick, Oil City, PA, April 3, 1980.

Witmer, Judith T. *Jebbie: Vamp to Victim,* Chapter 3. Hershey, PA: Yesteryear Press, 2011.

Women's Handbook, The Pennsylvania State College, 1924. (Section reprinted in *The Penn Stater*, July/August 2001, p. 45.)